JCISFA

Joint Center for International
Security Force Assistance

American Advisors

Security Force Assistance Model in the Long War

By Lieutenant Colonel Joshua J. Potter, US Army

2011

Published by Books Express Publishing
Copyright © Books Express, 2011
ISBN 978-1-780399-27-0

Books Express publications are available from all good retail and online booksellers. For
publishing proposals and direct ordering please contact us at: info@books-express.com

Author's Note

As a Special Forces and Civil Affairs Officer, I spent several years of my military career serving as an American advisor to a Foreign Security Force (FSF). Foreign Internal Defense (FID) proved to be one of the most rewarding experiences I could imagine. Most but not all of the segments and conversations described in this manuscript occurred in 2009-2010 between me and my Iraqi counterpart, who served as the Commanding General of the 17th Iraqi Army Division. I consider it an honored privilege to work with warriors of such high caliber and I am eternally grateful for Staff Major General Ali's friendship and mentorship during my fourth tour in Iraq. He convinced me that the Iraqi Nation will prevail on their own terms while benefitting from the countless sacrifices of our American Forces and our families.

Through proper application of our advisor programs, we can build the strongest tribe together.

First printing 2011

Abstract: This manuscript describes how US military advisors prepare for and conduct operations in war. Through two separate year-long combat tours as a military advisor in Iraq, the author brings true vignettes into modern military strategy and operational art. Further, the author provides multiple perspectives in command relationships. Through years of personal experience, direct interviews, and Warfighting knowledge, the author challenges conventionally accepted truths and establishes a new standard for understanding the impact of American advisors on the modern battleground.

Foreword

The Joint Center for International Security Force Assistance is pleased to introduce "American Advisors" by Lieutenant Colonel Josh Potter. Written while serving as the senior advisor to an Iraqi division commander as part of an Advise and Assist Brigade (AAB), this manuscript describes how US military advisors prepare for and conduct operations in war.

Through two, separate year-long combat tours as a military advisor in Iraq, Lieutenant Colonel Potter offers insights from the tactical operators and their foreign counterparts that capture the observations of the present in order to improve the quality of future American advisors. Further, the command relationships between the Advisor Team, US Battalion and or Brigade Combat Team (BCT), and the Foreign Security Force are explained from multiple perspectives. This publication is a must read for not only advisors but leaders of units preparing to conduct SFA and COIN in Iraq or Afghanistan.

Robert L. Caslen, Jr.
Lieutenant General, US Army
Director, JCISFA

Advise and Assist Brigade Commander Comments by

Roger Cloutier, Colonel, US Army, Commander, 1st Advise and Assist Brigade,
3d Infantry Division

The US Army published the Security Force Assistance (SFA) manual, FM 3-07.1 in May of 2009. Slated as the first fully resourced Advise and Assist Brigade (AAB) to deploy into Iraq, the Army augmented our Heavy Brigade Combat Team (HBCT) with a full complement of 48 advisors from December 2009 through December 2010. What lies in the pages that follow is a compendium of experiences from one of the six Iraqi Security Force Divisions we partnered with. Not all were as successful as the 17th Iraqi Army (IA) Division but the lessons learned there echoed across the Operating Environment (OE).

The role of the AAB Commander is to provide the guidance and operational leadership across the entire formation rather than direct specific action. We were going into the heart of the most dangerous country on the planet and we could not afford any leaders straying from the path. At times I had o interject directly in order to fix a problem, make good on a promise, or crush any idea that we were operating autonomously. We instilled the mantra that "As an AAB, we are junior partners in the relationship" and that, "The ISF success is our AAB success." These thoughts were revolutionary for our type-A personalities to grasp initially but became routine and elementary when we saw the proof that our Iraqi brothers were clearly up to the task.

As the advisors filtered into our formations, we evaluated them on paper, balancing their backgrounds between combat arms and operational support specialties. We tested them during our pre-deployment training scenarios. Following our rotation at the National Training Center (NTC), I talked candidly to my Task Force Commanders in order to see who would best work within the Command. We reformed the Stability-Transition Teams (S-TTs) and integrated them into our formation and guided them each step until they learned to walk in the light of our AAB mission. Then, we monitored them continuously to ensure they stayed on the straight path.

Our Advisors lived and worked with their counterparts – there was no compromise to this, as they had to build rapport and personal relationships with their Iraqi counterparts.

In order to promote unity of Command, we had to be creative. The US Task Force Commanders were, at times responsible for partnering with multiple Iraqi Divisions each exceeding 11,000 Iraqi *shurta* or *jundi*. We aligned our organization with the existing ISF boundaries, forsaking the traditional use of physical terrain to mark our organizational boundaries. Where other AABs experienced the tyranny of distance, the 1/3 AAB faced the daunting task of partnering with six ISF Divisions and three operational and area commands. In order to meet this challenge, I attached the S-TTs and legacy Military Transition Teams (MiTTs) to the Task Force Commanders. The Task Force Commanders normally provided a Company or Troop in Direct Support to the S-TTs. The MiTTs fell under the Administrative Control (ADCON) of the S-TTs as well. This provided little flexibility for our AAB in terms of uncommitted resources that could flex where we needed especially considering that in the same OE, seven US Brigades once occupied the capital province.

Our Soldiers served with distinction and honor during this tour as an AAB and our Iraqi brothers dutifully protected their homes and their people. We enabled the ISF to demonstrate their continued excellence and built their professional capacity and agile battle command.

The term "AAB" is a verb and not a noun. We had to shift our organization fluidly and adjust it to suit our environment. Below are the maxims we learned as the year progressed:

- The AAB is a mindset shift in how we view ourselves, our partners, the environment and the enemy.

- The ISF are our battlespace; relationships are a "pacing item" which we track.

- The entire organization of the brigade is in support the S-TT.

- Uniquely organized to meet environmental requirements; AABs will not look the same across the board.

- AABs must see the ISF better than they see themselves; we are an OC-like network that actively participates with the ISF.

- Agile Battle Command through combined operations centers are a way to both train the Iraqi staff as well as maintain situational awareness as less US forces are out in the Operating Environment (OE).

Did we solve each challenge? No. Did we disrupt the violent extremist networks (VEN)? You bet – and the Iraqi Security Forces were leading intelligence-driven precision counter-terrorism operations with our Advisor Support Teams (ASTs) by the ninth month of our rotation.

No one demonstrated greater success than Staff Major General Ali Jassim Al-Firaji and his leadership in the 17th IA Division.

Read the accounts of what the 17th IA Division, Task Force 2-7 Infantry, and their American Advisors did in the Southern Baghdad Belt and how they reshaped the once-feared "Triangle of Death." As we reduced the presence of the US Soldiers in the provincial capital of Baghdad, we consolidated our efforts and carefully selected where to apply our limited support.

Acknowledgements

I would like to dedicate this manuscript to our past, present, and future military and cultural advisors as well as our counterparts. To the countries we serve and the Soldiers we lead, thank you. We are your shadows.

Thank you to my wife Tracey and my children who have watched me pack and deploy several times. Such is the life of a Soldier. This manuscript may help make sense of what we do when we are so far away from the ones we love most. You remain my grace. Though this document is written by a single author, without the patience, knowledge, experience, and assistance of a truly talented team of dedicated professionals it is impossible to collect the evidence and put it all on paper. With this in mind, I wish to thank several organizations and units with particular attention to the key leaders who were instrumental in supporting this project.

- 17th Iraqi Army Division: Staff Major General Ali Jassim Muhammed Hassan Al-Firaji

- Combined Arms Center: Lieutenant General Robert L. Calsen, Lieutenant General William B. Caldwell IV

- Joint Center for International Security Force Assistance (JCISFA): Colonel Michael J. Swanson, Mr. Floyd Lucas, Major Tom Chalkley, Mr. Mark Lauber

- US Army / Marine Corps Counterinsurgency Center: Colonel Dan Roper

- 1st Infantry Division: General Carter Hamm, Major General (R) John Batiste, Major General Dana J.H. Pittard, Major General Vincent K. Brooks, Colonel (R) James Stockmoe, Colonel Jeffrey Ingram, Colonel Eric J. Wesley, Lieutenant Colonel Keith Casey, Colonel (R) Keith Cooper, Lieutenant Colonel Larry Shepherd

- 1st Armored Division: Major General Terry A. Wolff, Brigadier General Kevin W. Mangum, Brigadier General Kenneth E. Tovo, Brigadier General Ralph O. Baker, Brigadier General Glenn C. Hammond III

- 3d Infantry Division: Major General Tony Cucolo III, Brigadier General Jeffrey E. Phillips, Brigadier General Thomas S. James, Colonel Roger L. Cloutier, Lieutenant Colonel Gregory F. Sierra, Captain Kevin Murnyack, The Deathriders of D/2-7 Infantry

- 162d Infantry Training Brigade: Colonel Mark A. Bertolini, Lieutenant Colonel David M. Wood, Lieutenant Colonel Curtis B. Hudson, Major John Horning

- Center for New American Security (CNAS): Dr. John A. Nagl

- COIN Center - Kabul, Afghanistan: Lieutenant Colonel Mark Ulrich

- NATO Joint Forces Training Center: Lieutenant Colonel Chris Cardoni

- National Training Center (NTC): Brigadier General Robert B. Abrams, COL Ted Martin

- Center for Army Lessons Learned (CALL): Colonel (R) Rick Everett

- Peacekeeping Stability Operations Institute (PKSOI): Mr. Bill Flavin, Mr. Todd Wheeler

- US Special Operations Command (USSOCOM): Master Sergeant (R) Mike Beemer

- Battle Command Knowledge System (BCKS): Mr. Vince Carlisle, Mr. Ron Pruyt, Mr. Maurice Baggson, Mr. Bob Fox, Mr. Patrick Bremser, Lieutenant Colonel (R) Stephen Frank

- Battle Command Training Program (BCTP): Lieutenant Colonel Michael Landers

- Army Research Institute (ARI): Dr. Angela Karrasch, Dr .Michelle Zbylut

- Kansas State University (KSU): Mr. Daryl Youngman

- Fellow STTs, MiTTs, ETTs and OMLTs in Iraq and Afghanistan who serve honorably and contribute to our common defense

Through your sacrifice and dedication, we have preserved the hard lessons and blazed the trail forward. Thank you, all.

No worries

Contents

Figures

Prologue

The troops braved the icy February morning in order to catch a glimpse of the new military advisor who just came into the camp and was now talking through an interpreter to the Commander. The troops appeared less than impressed.

Upon seeing the well dressed military advisor, one soldier remarked, "Who does this officer think he is, wearing such a fine uniform? Doesn't he know most of us have only parts of a uniform?"

Another soldier responded, "I heard he spent some time on a general's staff in his own country, looks like he should go back there. This savagery will tear the badges off his uniform."

Figure 1: (From right to left) tribal sheik, interpreter, and US Advisor listening to Iraqi Army discussions of the security challenges in the Mahmudiyah Qada (region of southern Baghdad, in 2010.

"He looks old, at least 40. I wonder if he has ever seen combat," a young troop states.

An older soldier chimes in, "He probably heard some gunfire once and got himself a medal for it." Some of the soldiers snicker.

"Look at him. He has never seen a harsh winter like this. He probably wears two pairs of socks." The soldiers look sober, aware that most are not wearing socks but rags or paper in their shoes.

"I heard him speak earlier. He doesn't even know our language! What are we expected to learn from someone who cannot talk to us?"

A young officer responds, "Well, we are in contact with our enemy and our enemies are tyrants. So, while the enemy terrorizes our people, we are ordered to go through remedial training with this guy? His government may be worse than who we are fighting. Marvelous."

Over subsequent weeks, the opinions of this advisor changed. He proved to be an asset in every sense. He cursed at times (through his interpreter) when subordinates did not follow his orders but he clearly had a firm grasp on combat training and helped the units adjust to the battlefield. Under his tutelage, the army became more professional and disciplined.

The impressions of this past American advisor…

The advisor's poor command of the host nation language was a temporary hindrance because he had the prerequisite knowledge and experience.

He had another quality in a practical application of the host nation's character, remarkable for a man that had been in the country for so brief a time.

If he were to achieve anything with them, he would have to take a different approach than he would with his own countrymen.

He understood their character and adjusted his teaching methods accordingly.

Through a combination of charm, intimidation, and calculated theatrics, he earned their respect and affection and all this he did in the space of less than three months.

This particular advisor however was not serving in Iraq, Afghanistan, or the Philippines. He served in the American colonies from 1777-1784, as a foreign-born military advisor to the fledgling Continental Army. He was Baron Friedrich von Steuben, who arrived in the American colonies with no additional Prussian forces, only a letter of introduction from Benjamin Franklin, for the sole purpose of training the struggling and un-disciplined Continental Army. While sharing the miserable circumstances of a Continental Army Soldier fighting for independence from British rule, von Steuben indoctrinated the young army in terms of drills, movements, tactics, camp design, and even field sanitation. He began training a model company of 100 men who, in turn, trained the other Brigades in Valley Forge. This "train-the-trainer" concept was not new but it worked brilliantly and reinforced his exploits on the battlefield which earned the respect of the men he fought alongside.

Our recent experiments and experience with military advising have forced us to re-learn past lessons. We have re-discovered our own past adventures with advising from the Revolutionary War era of the 1770s and brought them into sharp focus for our present day combat advisors.

"Security force assistance is not new for the Army. In fact, General George Washington's Inspector General of the Army acted as an advisor for the Army. Baron Friedrich Wilhelm von Steuben instilled discipline and professionalism into an army that previously lacked formalized training. His 1779 Regulations for the Order and Discipline of the Troops of the United States, adapted from the Prussian army, formed the doctrinal backbone of the Continental Army throughout the Revolutionary War. Additionally, the lineage of the Army's operations field manual, FM 3-0, can be traced to this document. As a benefactor of advisors such as von Steuben, the Army has since undertaken what is called security force assistance on numerous occasions throughout its history."

-- FM 3-07.1, SFA Chapter 4

It is important to note that our own prized army was born from a revolutionary spirit, and professionalized from Prussian and French combat advisors. The classic examples embodied in Baron von Steuben and the Marquise de Lafayette are stark reminders of the debt we owe to our European allies. Without their assistance, technical expertise, and their countries' outright support, we well could have lost our own bid for independence more than 200 years ago. These two men had a dramatic effect upon our professional army (note: we live with a professional army not conscripted from the masses and we have no compulsory military service obligations).

Further, we are continually learning where and how to apply ourselves and how to adapt to our surroundings, to be successful on the battlefields. The best advisors are often the best students and those willing to learn from their counterparts rather than applying stale, prescribed, comfortable military Tactics, Techniques, and Procedures (TTPs) in the face of unfamiliar and foreign challenges.

Today we are militarily engaged in several countries, not all of them in direct combat operations. We remain, however an Army at war, from our hearts and to our muddy boots. Some of the fiercest fighting done alongside our Foreign Security Force (FSF) counterparts is in the same manner British military advisor T.E. Lawrence fought in the Arabian Peninsula during the World War I. He collected his thoughts and wisdom in a monumental tome nearly a century ago. We owe our combat advisor heroes of today the same recognition and understanding of their lessons through the next century.

"I need to prepare for problems I don't know exist yet."
Colonel Peter Newell, Commander, 4th BCT, 1st Armored Division

The above quote is from Colonel Newell's comments on his responsibility to train his BCT as the Proof of Principle for the Advise and Assist Brigade (AAB) concept (also called a Brigade Combat Team and Augmented for Security Force Assistance, or BCT-A), across three provinces and two Iraqi Security Force Divisions in southern Iraq.

Section I

The Characters

The General: The Commanding General of the 17th Iraqi Army Division (over 10,000 strong) is responsible for the security of 500,000 people in the southern belt of Baghdad between the Tigris and Euphrates Rivers. The General was born in Karkh district of Baghdad in 1969, the son of a prominent tribal sheik, and served in the Iraqi Army as an officer in the previous regime. He left military service in 2003 and returned in 2004. Though he is a Shi'a Muslim, the General married a Sunni Muslim and he is a non-sectarian professional warrior.

The US AAB Commander: The Commander of the 1st Brigade, 3rd Infantry Heavy Brigade Combat Team (HBCT) is the first fully resourced Advise and Assist Brigade (AAB) in Iraq (December 2009 and January 2011). This AAB received 24 Stability-Transition Teams (S-TT, each composed of two field grade officers) to provide the core of the advisor tasks. The AAB task organized their four maneuver Battalions into Task Forces who partnered with a total of six Iraqi Army Divisions. Additionally, the AAB was responsible for advising three area commands (the Baghdad Operations Center, Karkh Area Command and Rusafa Area Command). This meant 1/3 AAB was tasked to validate the fully resourced AAB concept in the crucible. The 1/3 AAB was solely responsible for enabling the ISF to secure their capital province.

The US Task Force Commander: The Commander of Task Force 2-7 Infantry, is partnered with the 17th Iraqi Army Division and (six months into deployment) also the 6th Iraqi Army Division, who controls 80% of western and southern Baghdad.

The Division Advisor (author): The S-TT Chief, for 17th IA Division is responsible for the 17th IA Division S-TT and directing three subordinate Brigade S-TTs (23rd IA Brigade, 25th IA Brigade and 55th IA Brigade), who have their own IA Commanders as counterparts.

The *jundi*, or *jenood*: "Soldiers" of the Iraqi Army (IA).

The *shurta*: "Policemen" of the Iraqi Police Services (IPS).

The *sawah*: Members of the Concerned Local Citizens (CLCs) and are a para-military, civil defense force authorized as part of a reconciliation effort to carry weapons and conduct checkpoint operations which assist in providing security to the rural roads and outlying tribally-controlled areas. They're also known as "Sons of Iraq (SoI)".

The sheiks: 14 main tribal sheiks in this area. These "blood sheiks," are those with hereditary honor to serve and represent their tribes. There are over 5,000 sub-sheiks in the area too.

The enemy: *Irhabee* or terrorists and *mujarim* or criminals. The enemy fights against the people and the security forces for their own benefit (political power, money, or revenge).

The people: Approximately 500,000 people (Sunni and Shia) live in Mahmudiyah Qada, the region also known as the Southern Baghdad Belt, once named "the Triangle of Death."

1

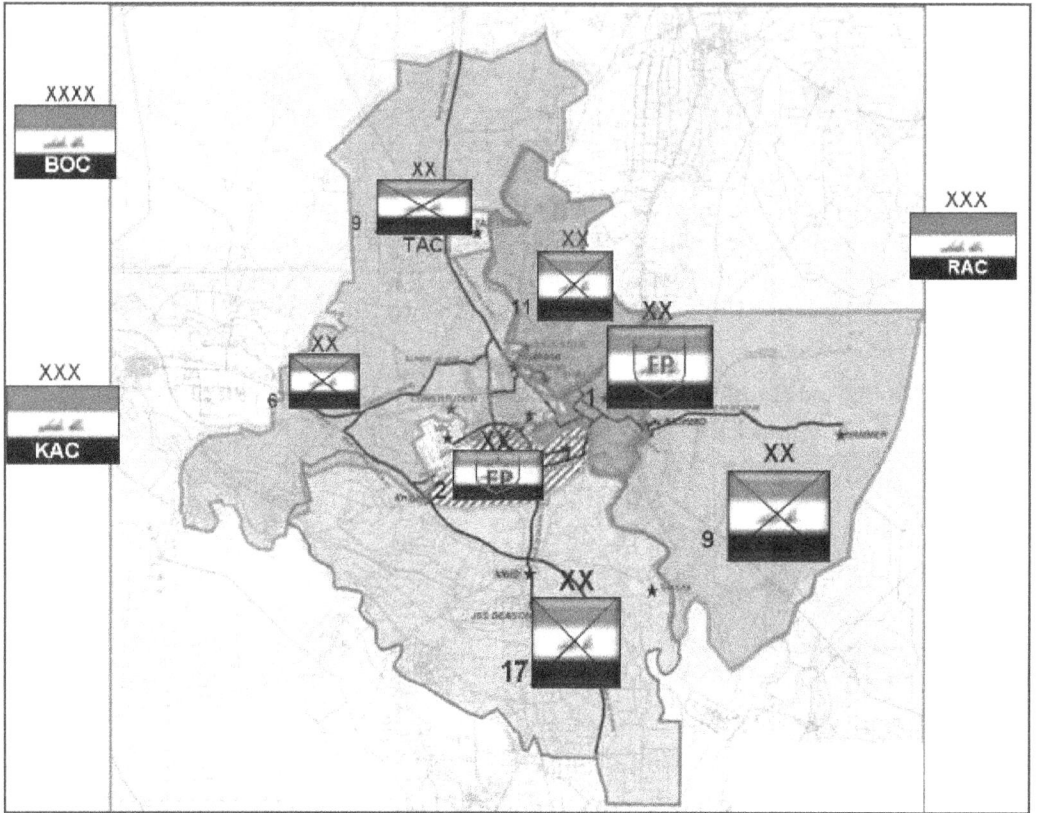

Figure 2. General Iraqi Security Force (ISF) disposition in Baghdad Province. 17th IA division area of responsibility is the Mahmudiyah Qada region of southern Baghdad, 2010.

Section II

Advisor and FSF Counterpart Exchanges

Figure 3. The general's Office. We spent 30 percent of our time together in this room.

I knock discretely on the open door and progress cautiously, although the general's aide assured me the general is in a good mood this morning. It is 11 o'clock in the morning and late by US standards but I was up with the general until past midnight the evening before. Cigarette smoke fills the air of the opulent office as we enter. The general looks up from the scores of papers, folders, and binders heaped upon his desk and smiles, apparently glad for the reprieve from the paperwork on his ornate desk. He appears older than his 40 years of age and the wisdom and pressure of command is apparent in the air surrounding him. Still, he looks as rested as I could hope. I salute as he motions for us to come and sit.

It is 12 paces from the office door to the couch next to the general's desk. The office is spacious, adorned with dozens of large photos on the wall of the general with influential people who have visited him and gifts from previous US units. Gold trim accents most of the woodwork and marble and glass tea tables stand in front of the dozen or so chairs and sofas lining the walls. We speak cordially in Iraqi Arabic, as my understanding is limited to simple common words and phrases.

3

"*Asal'am al-lakum, sadee,* [Hello, sir]" I say smiling, as I enter.

"*Wa-alakum sal'lam, Abu* Damon [which is to say 'Hello father of Damon']," he responds in a familiar tone. He smiles and extends his hand for a firm handshake as he stands. '*Abu* Damon,' is his name for me when things are going well. When disturbed by something, he addresses me by my rank and last name '*Muqadim* Potter' [Lieutenant Colonel Potter]. That is when I know to watch my step and to listen before I speak as something is disturbing him which we will need to discuss before anything else. So, with these gestures and first words, I know this is a low threat meeting and I do not expect an ambush.

Before I am permitted to sit, I shake his hand with both of mine. Sometimes I will accompany this handshake with a kiss over his cheek. This is the respectful custom for our greeting and an honor. He greets me first and then my interpreter, a stalwart Iraqi-American named "Jim." My deputy Team Chief, Major Barry Horsey, repeats the greetings with the general too. He is my witness and my conscience in every engagement.

"*Straya* [sit]," offers the general.

"*Shukran, sadee* [thank you, sir]," I respond. I sit on the couch closest to the general on his right side, as he prefers. Jim sits on my right and close, as he is well trusted and respected by both the general and me. Several times, Jim has helped both of us sort through how to ask for help and how to understand the other. Jim is more of a cultural advisor for both of us rather than a simple mouthpiece. Our Deputy Team Chief sits close enough to hear Jim and to record any agreements we make. He is a diligent complex problem solver who speaks quietly and offers each of us in the room professional counsel and a sounding board when we need it. The general jokes, "You and Major Horsey share a brain." This is precisely what he should do. The general knows this and understands that anything he says to me, I will discuss with Major Horsey later. There are no secrets between us.

As we sit, the general offers, "*Allah bukhair*" [May God bless this meeting].

"*Allah bukhair*!" we both respond, as Jim and I place our right hand over our hearts and then in the air as a simple wave. This gesture is the acknowledgment as if saying something from the heart.

The general is pleased, as the evening before, his unit seized a terrorist based on the information the American unit provided for his forces. He presses the electric door bell on his desk. The soft ding dong in the next office summons a young man in civilian clothes, a friend's nephew, I am told later.

"*Jeep chai* [bring tea]," commands the general. The assistant stomps his foot in the doorway, acknowledging the order, and scurries out.

The general reaches into the folds of his shirt and pulls out his cigarettes. Marlboro lights are his brand of choice. He smokes about two to three packs per day and I wonder what he can taste anymore. His voice is raspier than his 40 years would suggest and our US doctors have examined him but the physicians maintain, despite his unhealthy smoking habit, he is as healthy as can be. The general happily lights up.

He offers me a cigarette which I accept, though I have told him I prefer cigars. I know the general hates cigar smoke, so I refuse to smoke the fine cigars my wife and friends send to me if he is around. Cigars are a personal pleasure I enjoy while deployed and "It keeps the girls away from us," I tell my wife, who only permits me to smoke cigars when deployed and never at home. The general passes me his lighter. He does not light the cigarette for me as it would be a gesture of subordination and nor do I light his cigarette. I join him smoking as the *chai* arrives.

"*Shlonek, Abu* Damon? [How are you?],"he asks, as he stirs the sugar from the bottom of the small *chai* glass, clinking the spoon against the side of the glass. He notices the large, unsealed manila envelope in my lap which contains the intelligence reports (all "REL IRQ," or 'Releasable to the Iraqi Security Forces') gathered over the last 12 hours and translated into Arabic with key locations printed on small maps or imagery.

"*Kula zayn, hamdal'allah! Wa inta, sadee*? [Very well, thanks be to God! And you, sir?]" I sip the scalding, hot *chai*, preferring not to stir in all of the sugar. I have seen enough diabetic Iraqi Generals to understand that sugar is silently destroying this vibrant society.

"*Zayn, zayn*. [Good, good.]," He smiles thinly and breathes out the smoke as if it was the stress impressed upon his body from the incalculable amount of pressure he is routinely under.

"So," he begins in English. He reaches out his hand for the morning intelligence reports. "We are good, you and I. Now, we have work to do." The general smiles and the day begins.

This is our daily routine. We have been together for weeks and months, establishing a rhythm for each day's responsibilities. We know each other's moods and how to work with the other and, most importantly, how to be respectful of the other. We know each other's sleep cycle and how to maximize the use of our time together. This comes from a genuine respect for each other and a sincere desire to improve our relationship.

The general is responsible for all security forces in the area to include army, police, and *sawa* or facilities protective services and it's his phone which rings first if an IED detonates. Professionally, I am his American advisor and he is an division commander in the Iraqi Army. Personally, we are friends who enjoy working together towards many of the same goals in support of our nations' common defense.

Ego has no place for a good advisor. This job has cost some measure of personal and professional pride but, as my pastor reminds me, pride is a sin. So I suppose humility is not a poor trait for an advisor to express. It is difficult for me however, as I am not a humble person by nature. My wife can attest to this.

My job here is to assist the Iraqi division commander improve the security for the 500,000 citizens of Southern Baghdad and do so in a manner consistent with our American values and rules of conduct. This is not such a tough job and in fact, I absolutely love it! It is ambiguous enough to be exciting each day where we measured results by the faces we work with. I do not know enough Arabic to carry on an in depth conversation but I have been around Iraqis long enough after four tours of duty to understand a limited vocabulary and read their body language, gestures, tone, and expressions in order to determine whether we are doing the right things and building a positive relationship, or whether we are being played and taken advantage of and which would be a betrayal to our wounded and fallen brothers who have sacrificed so much for the freedoms that the Iraqi people now enjoy.

In essence, this is a job I feel uniquely suited for. Leading a small unit in a combat advisor capacity is more fun than a barrel of monkeys! So, there are several questions we are asked, as American advisors:

What do the advisors do?

How do the advisors do it? (How *should* the advisors do it?)

How do we train to be advisors?

What are the differences between partnering and advising?

Is an advisor position worth distinguishing the effort?

What is the benefit to getting this relationship right?

How do our counterparts see us?

How do we measure effective success? How do our counterparts measure success?

What is our impact upon the indigenous population?

How do we work as an interagency towards common goals?

Where do we want to be in five or 10 years?

Who is responsible for implementing organizational change?

What is the future for American advisors?

These are the questions we will discuss and more. Do we provide all of the answers… yes! (Just kidding)

Of course each situation is different and what applied and worked well in one particular area and time may not work in the same area at a different time. The success and failures of advisor efforts are functions of many variables and include some ridiculously difficult factors to predict such as mood, personality, agitation, and other human factors. The examples used in this document are factual and they happened. Not all of these examples and vignettes ended well. We are not always successful. However, I believe we should improve from our successes and learn from our mistakes, lest we repeat them.

To begin, there are several roles which American advisors must adopt. When embedded directly with our Foreign Security Force (FSF) counterpart unit, we are the most effective when we eat with them, sleep with them, work with them, and fight alongside them. Without embedding, the perils of advising compounds exponentially by each kilometer that separates our sleeping areas with those of the FSF. In short, each hour you are not with your counterpart is an hour you have no direct and immediate impact. This does not mean we have to remain at each other's side 24/7 but commuting to the fight is not a good option either. The optimal time and exposure lies between those extremes.

Figure 4. Combined planning session and ISF brief during a combined rehearsal in 2007. Note, ISF, US Partner units, and US advisors participate while local nationals look on in the background.

Advisors socialize concepts between the US and FSF units. We are Americans first but must continuously inform the US partner units as to what is driving the FSF organization. This is also a two way street for information. Often times, the FSF Commander will propose an idea to a trusted advisor before his own staff or subordinate commanders, the same way we float potential advice through our professional confidants and deputies. The FSF commander wants to think through the decision and predict possible outcomes before issuing a command. Often in the FSF military culture we work in, asking for help or analysis is considered weakness or not aggressive enough. A good advisor will keep the lines of communication open at all times and play the role of confidant to both sides, which the advisor earns by maintaining trust and respect for discretion when discussing details of a personal matter or sensitive limitation. Again, remember we are Americans first and a stranger in a strange land, looking to advise and assist and not to be assimilated (refer to "going native" in the Perils of Advising section).

Advisors synthesize information from both the US and FSF into a workable hybrid solution. This compromise is an attempt to balance strengths from one side and to cover the challenges of the other side. Moreover, the advisor must ensure the final plan is moving towards the same or common goal.

Advisors **do not need** to honestly be subject matter experts (SME) in their field. So long as an advisor is technically and tactically proficient in their given field, they can be effective. Few advisors are true experts in anything. The ability to build and maintain a positive relationship is of paramount importance when working to earn cultural competence with a FSF counterpart. Technical expertise is a rare commodity and may actually inhibit good advising, if the expert's ego gets in the way of working a sustainable hybrid solution.

For example, think of a doctor with a horrible bedside manner and say is a highly respected cardiologist to whom you've been referred due to serious chest pain. You may not like the cardiologist but he is the expert in his field. You are apt to listen to his diagnosis but spurn his advice and even at the expense of your own health if the guy is a jackass. You are more likely to listen and apply similar advice on "eating well and exercising as preventive health" from someone who works with you and has known you for years, even if he isn't a well published cardiologist. Relationships matter, particularly when offering advice across military subcultures.

Technical advisors called forward to train the FSF on a particular weapon system or skills serve as SMEs. The FSF expects them to be a SME. This technical advising is subtly different than more conventional military advising and because of the need to know the answers and to be able to effectively communicate. An effective conventional advisor may simply possess the ability to assist the FSF to work through their issues in order to arrive at a sustainable solution. So, how should advisors gain sincere rapport quickly?

Good advisors, just as neighbors and friends, eat with your counterparts. Sharing meals is a cultural necessity. This means you may have to forgo some things you detest and try to enjoy the local fare. For example, I despise pickled fish, which unfortunately for me, was a staple food in Kosovo and Russia when I worked there. It was terrible. God bless the vodka and *rakia* my host served alongside the fish!

While in Iraq and Afghanistan, we eat what our counterparts eat. It's actually quite good, as shown in the photos. If you leave a table hungry after a meal with your counterpart, it's your own damned fault.

Also, table etiquette is one of the first lessons you should receive from your local national interpreters and we say local nationals because they are the best cultural advisors for the advisor team and it is in their best interest that you do not embarrass yourself or your country by committing a social *faux pas* during your initial engagements. Every meeting is considered an "engagement". For example, you should know when to wash your hands and whether eating with utensils is permissible and how to navigate eating off a communal plate.

In 2004, I recall my initial surprise during a meal at a tribal sheik's home when he grabbed a slab of sheep from a large communal plate and placed it on the table in front of me. No forks, no plates, and no worries. Our interpreter had previously informed me that Iraqis considered it a great honor to be served in this manner by the host of the meal. I recommend people from the west quickly shed the initial revulsion of other's bare hands touching our food under such circumstances. After all, the sheep tasted good and we needed the support of the tribal sheik in order to peacefully relocate his tribe in a new area.

Meals are as much a test to your social aptitude as the appearance of your uniform, which reflects military professionalism. There are lists of "do's and don'ts" for eating with your FSF counterpart and every culture is different. Talk to the local nationals (interpreters) first and know what to expect. Have a cultural meal as part of your training and practice your social etiquette as it is important to make a good first impression.

Figure 5. US advisors eating cow brains with Afghan National Security Force counterparts 2009.

Next, advisors share risk and fight alongside their counterparts. This means sharing base defense responsibilities not subjugating your security to your counterparts or vice versa. This means combined patrols, combined operations centers, and sharing ammunition in a firefight if you have the same caliber weapons. Shoulder-to-shoulder and back-to-back, there should be no daylight between you and your counterparts when hunting the enemy.

The single most rewarding point of my military career to date occurred in February of 2006 when rather than shooting an insurgent who was firing an AK-47 from behind a tree in a palm grove 250 meters away, I pointed out the guy to the Iraqi lieutenant crowding my hard cover. I coached the lieutenant on the AK-47 range about a week before and knew he could get this guy who was shooting at us. I waved the command to cease-fire to the rest of the US advisor team next to us and the insurgent poked his head out and started spraying rounds in our direction. I coached the lieutenant , who took a few deep breaths and shot the terrorist high in the shoulder on the third shot. "*Kulah zayhn!* [Very good!]," I exclaimed, as the young lieutenant beamed. The enemy gunman went down hard.

I turned around and saw the slack jawed Iraqi battalion commander, who was my FSF counterpart at the time say, "*Hamda'allah!* [Thanks be to God!]." That Iraqi lieutenant went on to command the battalion commander's Personal Security Detail the following day and every day after. The lieutenant stood immediately at my side during each dangerous mission we faced. Military advising is best during combat operations, in my humble opinion, not because of elevated serotonin levels or type-A personality but because the results of the work are immediate, resolute, and powerful.

For an example of how to work and fight with your FSF counterpart, build a combined tactical standing operating procedure (TACSOP). Each country is different of course, and each unit within the country is just as varied when conducting things such as combined operations. We have included considerations for a refined S-TT TACSOP (See Appendix A: S-TT Tactical SOP - TACSOP) at the end of this book.

Play with your counterpart too. If you are having fun in war, you chose the wrong job. Play soccer. Play basketball. Play pool. Play cards. Some of the best conversations I have had with my FSF counterparts were during a game of cards. During those times, the counterpart will decompress and allow a few select people near him to relax with.

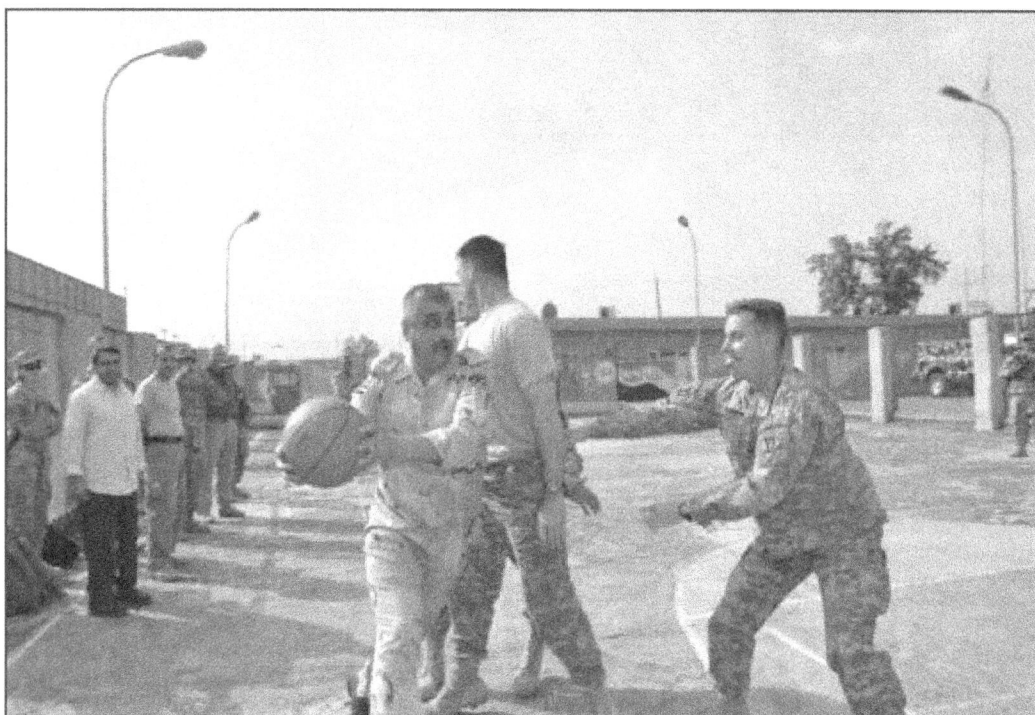

Figure 6. The general, the advisor (screening), and the partner unit relaxing on the court before lunch.

"*Abu* Damon, let us teach you this game called '*khan kan* [51]'." The general explains the card game through Jim. It takes about two minutes to explain the rules and then I study the players. I stay quiet, watching the cards and the players, not to look for 'tells' but to see who the general considers his closest comrades. Jim provides me with the details of how to arrange your hand and when to throw away a garbage card without feeding your opponent. We were called at 9:30 p.m. and asked to join his card game this evening. My deputy chief and I arrived on time at 10:00 p.m. but the general had to "wrap-up a few matters in Baghdad and was late returning," according to his aide-de-camp.

By around 11:00 p.m., the general was finally in a comfortable track suit, smoking a signature cigarette, drinking *chai,* and laughing with his men in his villa. The card game was played with four people and in addition to the general, the other players were his commando battalion commander, the garrison commander, and another lieutenant colonel that we had noticed around the headquarters building but had no idea of his duty or job. His division logistician (G4) was there too, waiting on a couch with his arms around several binders and he appeared nervous. Likely, the general asked to review his hand receipts book again. The general was a meticulous man with his official record and can spot an error without opening the book, if he makes the Division G4 wait and stress long enough.

We all remained in complete military uniform despite the general's comfy tracksuit. There was a lesson in that alone and tonight we paid careful attention.

In my mind, the card game *khan kan* was a cross between playing spades with a partner and gin rummy (mixing suits, straights, and runs of cards). The game was easy to learn but tough to keep score. This was only the second time I had been invited to the general's villa where he spends his few relaxing hours when he is not a work. This was his sanctuary and all are respectful and quiet when they are here. It was almost hallowed ground to the Iraqis and the impact of the invitation was not lost on me.

During the next two hours, we did not directly discuss work at all. We discussed the cards, our families, past missions, and humorous "war stories". It was a chance for the general to see who I was, how I behaved, and what I truly wanted. It was a chance for me to get to know the general's closest allies and to learn what motivated them through their history together. It was a card game to see how well we paid attention to each other.

We learned who the general respected. We learned who let the general win and how he knew it. We learned who despised my apparent favor with the general and earned some reluctant acceptance by them. We learned to keep our trap shut and listen. During the final hand of the eighth game, the general smiled as he showed me his cards and it was a perfect hand, a straight flush of 14 cards in sequence. The metaphor was not lost on me either.

Following the game, the other three players saluted and left. The general turned to his logistician, "Are you still here?" he asked, feigning surprise.

A little dejected and humbled, "*Na'am, Sadee* [yes, sir]," responded the G4. He knew damned well he was sitting there with beads of sweat rolling down his face and down his neck. For hours the G4 was thinking through the reports and periodically opening one of the binders and making a carefully scribbled correction or annotation.

"Show me the reports," commanded the general. He snatched the books away and irritatingly swept away the sweat from the G4's hands that stained the top binder.

"Where are the errors?" inquired the general, without opening the book.

"I have fixed the errors, *sadee*…All of them," responded the G4 with a cracking voice. The general peered at the G4's face closely.

"How many errors do you have to make before you give me an accurate report?!" scolded the general.

The G4 appeared panicked and began to make excuses for things the general didn't know about. The general escalated the discussion by asking more probing questions and only scanned the information on the pages of the tabbed binders.

"Are you a lieutenant?! No, you are a lieutenant colonel and my logistics officer, responsible for drawing and equipping my division. When you fail, I know. It reflects upon me and this division when you fail. I get called to explain why the equipment we asked for and begged for months ago was not drawn properly. Your failure would damage us all." The general shook the man's confidence with the reprimand.

"*Sadee*, it wasn't my fault," the G4 began. "We couldn't draw the vehicles immediately because the ministry wanted to send some of the vehicles to other units. I…"

"You should be waiting at the ministry now to get the 20 vehicles they promised us!" interrupted the general. "Now, only through my contacts will we able to fix the problems you caused. I should not have to spend my *wasta* to fix your failures! Tomorrow, draw the remaining equipment and get it on a hand receipt. Be there at 9:00 a.m."

"But *sadee*, the warehouse does not open until 10:00 .a.m." The G4 fumbles as the words stream out of his mouth.

"Be there at 7:00 a.m., with all of the trucks to finish the draw. Call my aid from the warehouse telephone outside when you arrive." the general concludes and hands the unopened binder back to the G4. The general softens his tone in an attempt to reconcile the damage to the G4's ego, "I cannot stand another failure from you, *habibi* [my close friend]. Or I will punish you, understand?"

"*Na'am, sadee*. [yes, sir.] I am sorry…never again."

The general motions to dismiss the G4 and turns his back on him as the G4 stomps his foot and salutes at the doorway and leaves the villa.

The general rubs his hair, which I could swear was darker that morning. I say nothing and remained seated and motionless on the side of the room. Jim remains still as well.

The general lights another cigarette and inhales deeply. He motions me towards the door and we walk out together. We walk towards the gate which leads to the US compound. I remained quiet as we walk slowly.

"So, what do you think, *Abu* Damon?" His countenance is calmer and he looks at the ground as we walk. "It's an interesting game," I said. The general stops and looks directly at me. "You do not lay your cards on the table until you are ready to win, even though you could lay them down much earlier in the game. Your partner discards what he knows your opponents can't use and you play with multiple decks, which I am not used to. There is a lot going on during the game. I would like to learn more and I am not ready to play this game quite yet."

The general smiles and then laughs as he says, "Then you will come back later this week. I will call when we play. You are always welcome here." I salute and say, goodnight.

What did I learn...plenty. There was a lot more occurring behind the scenes than the information readily observed. The division G4 is one of the most powerful trusted men in this organization. He serves at the whim of the commander and is well connected. Offer advice when it's requested and earn the privilege to offer advice through building a personal and professional relationship. It would have been easy to jump on the G4 for his failures, to blame the patrol leader for not filling the fuel tanks of the vehicles. Or, advise about the importance of rehearsals, fuel expenditure projections, prior coordination, or updating the commander during the equipment draw operation. At the time, however, I didn't have enough information to make an assessment. A great battalion commander once told me, "Never pass up an opportunity to keep your mouth shut." How did I remain effective? I kept my mouth shut and listened. Sometimes the best advice I give is to me.

This all ties back to social interaction and professional study of your counterpart as an advisor. During our most recent duty as a combat advisor, we played cards, pool, chess, ping-pong, basketball, and soccer with our counterparts. Let there be no mistake, when you play, play fair and play to win. They would know if you are not playing your best. They want to beat you too but only in a good match.

In today's fights, we must exhibit operational patience, according to best practices training provided by the US Army and Marine Corps Counterinsurgency Center. This means we must resist the temptation to move in and assert ourselves. It may seem simple to "fix" an easy problem sometimes. However, when advising it is often best to take a listening pause to hear the whole problem and understand the relationships in play before offering advice or assistance. We do not want to generate more insurgents than we neutralize.

Be patient and listen. Advising is most effective behind closed doors in private conversations. While you are in the public eye, advising your counterpart may convey an image of weakness to your counterpart. Advising during a firefight is also ill-advised and when bullets are flying stay close to your counterpart and protect him but resist the warrior desire to take charge if it's not your fight. The advisor position is to fight alongside his counterpart and always stay close and fiercely protective.

Did the IA Division ever get the 20 vehicles that were promised? Yes and about 60 days later. It can take a long time to fulfill promises in this country despite the sincerest efforts.

Study the leadership style of your counterpart

The general is disturbed. I notice as I approach him. First off, he was not in his office at the usual time but we spotted him walking briskly between buildings in his headquarters base camp. I watched him from inside a building in our operations center. The general had a small group of men surrounding him furiously scribbling notes as the general walked into one building and then another, gesturing and giving animated directions neither I nor Jim could hear. The mannerisms were enough to demonstrate he was angry. We lost sight of the general as he moved into the garrison commander's office and didn't come out. Jim, my Deputy, and I went in after him a minute later. We had to ask some critical questions about the upcoming national elections and confirm the division was ready to secure all of the polling sites.

We listened carefully as we approached the closed door to the garrison commander's office. Normally doors stay open when the boss is around unless, of course, he is yelling at someone. We heard nothing as we knocked and entered. The general was sitting at the garrison commander's large desk. The general had remanded the garrison commander to the couch on the wall. The men stood as we greeted each other. After the brief pleasantries, the general got down to business.

"I have 47 officers in my division headquarters. Do you know how many I found actually working at 1:00 p.m. today? Three!" The general exclaimed in an exasperated tone. "Everyone else was either watching TV, reading books, sleeping, or eating. We will have our national elections tomorrow and they are acting lazy! This is ridiculous!"

"*Na'am, sadee* [yes, sir]," the garrison commander affirmed. He was not normally one to speak very much but his voice seemed to calm the general. "I know it seems too much. They are acting lazy and without supervision."

The garrison commander continued to me, "The duty officer last night conducted a routine inspection of the barracks for the Soldiers. Common Soldiers were not supposed to have any cell phones as they used to compromise time sensitive information. The duty officer found and confiscated 75 cell phones last night from the barracks. "

"Now, the battalion commander must make an investigation of the operational security measures and we will burn the 75 cell phones," the general said.

"I think the *jundi* [Soldiers] are going soft," responded the garrison commander.

"Exactly," said the general. "They should be looking for work and at least doing their jobs! If they have nothing to occupy them, I will find something. During the *Arba'een* pilgrimage, we had all extra officers running checkpoints along the 30 kilometer pilgrimage route. Maybe we need to send them out of the headquarters, to live on the streets."

I knew he was being vicious but it wasn't helping his blood pressure. He continued to vent for five minutes on the subject. He held a metal ruler in his hands and routinely made menacing gestures and tapped the desk with it.

Finally exasperated, the general lit a cigarette, looked at me and said, "*Shoku moku, Abu* Damon? [How's it going?]" I figured it was okay to speak honestly.

"I am disturbed, *sadee*," I began.

"*Layish*? [Why?]" asked the general.

"It's because I grew up with a teacher who used to smack your hands if you misbehaved with a ruler just like the one in your hands, now." I said. The general looked at the ruler and laughed a little.

"Well, as long as you don't misbehave, like some of my other officers, you are ok!" he said.

Returning his smile, I tried to disarm his anger with a subtle solution. "I am used to a system where the senior officers held the younger officers accountable for performing daily routines. I mean, you have a division to run and more than 10,000 men and you cannot watch everyone all the time. You have a span of about six sub-commanders you can directly control continuously. These are your brigade commanders, the division deputy commander and the division chief of staff [one-star generals], and a couple of special staff officers. That's enough to keep you busy, right?" The general nodded gestured for me to continue. "Every day an officer must make a contribution to the division and accomplish something, no matter how small or great. If the staff section officers are not performing, they must be accountable to the primary staff officer. If the primary staff officer is lazy, the chief of staff steps in and disciplines him. You cannot watch everyone all of the time. Just spot check and do a few routine checks with your key officers, the brigade commanders, and the other generals in the division."

The general picks up a ledger book. "You see this? We had a system where every day each officer had to record what they were doing, what progress they made, and what they would do the following day but if I didn't check it after five or six days, no one would fill out the reports! Why? They are lazy and did not want to contribute, as you say."

I decided not to push the issue and the general changed the subject. We continued the day inspecting the commando battalion which lifted the spirits of the general. His commando battalion was led well and training for combat. The battalion commander was a huge (easily 6 feet, 6 inches) Iraqi who was also a trusted confidant to the general and a great friend to our advisor team. The battalion commander expertly guided the general through his barracks, supply rooms, dining hall, and training areas. As expected, the general calmed down during the impromptu inspection, reassured that at least his commando battalion was gearing up for national elections properly.

After an hour of simmering, the general called his deputy division commander to meet with him. The boss expressed his displeasure of witnessing the sloth from the morning and directed that between "6:00 a.m. and 6:00 p.m., each staff officer will be assigned to a TCP or a polling site." They would make regular reports of the status of the site every two hours and ensure the soldiers and policemen treated people with respect while ensuring their security.

Later that night, the effects of that order were still buzzing around the headquarters. The Iraqis did not seem to understand why the general was so irritated. I explained to one officer, "Sometimes the medic needs to apply direct pressure to a wound when it is hemorrhaging, to control the bleeding." Moreover, I explained that it was unwise to criticize the general's decisions without cause and particularly to the general's primary US advisor. The officer agreed and returned to his duties.

This latter point brought another dimension of military advising into focus and the FSF will bring criticisms to you about just about everything. An advisor is a sounding board and many FSF folks will attempt to use the advisor to fix problems they are too weak, scared, incompetent, or otherwise unable to fix themselves. It is important to deflect those types of whiners. Let them know that you have a counterpart and the first response to understanding a problem is to ask, "What are you doing about it?" Too often, the FSF response is a sly smile and, "Well I am bringing the problem to YOUR attention 'Mr. Advisor' to solve it! We are not able to fix it ourselves." This is a typical lazy response. The advisor must redirect to the FSF to come up with a viable solution that we can assist them with as we cannot cure all of their ills. Moreover, if the problem in question is not a priority to the FSF Commander, we may be spinning our wheels to focus on it. Our ultimate goal is to formulate sustainable solutions and systems that work for the FSF and are independent of US enablers.

To this, we also gain the wisdom and experience from the US task force commander, who uses the maxim, "Don't fix the problem for your subordinates. Identify where the system is broken and fix that."

Interestingly, the general's favorite word is the same as the US task force commander, "*Layish?* [Why?]". With a series of operational requirements and limited assets, the commander always asks why something is required. This helps him and us to prioritize resources needed to accomplish truly important objectives. Simultaneously, when submitting a request for information, I am compelled to state why the information is important. Accordingly, we have respectfully declined answering spurious questions which are not tied to a higher commander's information requirement. Often, the staff officers of higher headquarters will ask a question or require a detailed assessment in an area which does not matter to the IA Command or the US Command. Asking, 'why?' or 'how will this information be used to drive a decision?' often alleviates pursuing a rabbit down its hole and wasting time. There is plenty of information that we need to sift through and advisors are not privy to everything. Once we build rapport with our counterpart, a professional relationship becomes personal quickly particularly when bullets are flying. We must try to use our influence where it will be mutually beneficial. Ask, "Why?"

Measures of Effectiveness

The general is shivering with a fever today with a bone wracking cough and pneumonia may be setting in. The stress of recent activity appears to be breaking down his body's immune system. Accordingly, we arranged with our partnering task force's physician to get him x-rays and a checkup at a nearby US installation. After performing a battlefield circulation with the US task force commander, the general rests in his office, directly under the heating vent of a wall-mounted air conditioner.

We are discussing the day's events when the lights go out. Within 15 seconds, the backup generator kicks on, restoring power. The general begins, "The Minister of Electricity recently stated in a public address that in 2003, before the war with the Coalition Forces, Baghdad used about five megawatts of electricity per day. There were few air conditioners and most middle-upper class income households had less than two window-mounted A/C units." "Today, in Baghdad," the general continues, "with average homes using four or five A/C units, the city consumes more than 12,000 megawatts of electricity. How can we keep up?!"

"Exactly," I respond. "The demand has increased, and the expectations of the people have changed. They expect essential services to support a better quality of life."

This was a typical exchange with a tough answer.

Simply put, how do we know we are achieving positive results? How do we measure the success?

A good friend of mine explained that US forces are masters of reporting our performance but rely on the FSF to measure our effectiveness. A measure of performance indicates how well we are doing our job ("We conducted 18 combined patrols this week," or "We trained five IA soldiers on how to use a Harris radio"). Measures of effectiveness indicate a change in system behavior ("During the combined patrols this week, we received four walk-up sources with tips that paid-off," or "The IA has established their own HF communications shot using Harris radios to support their communications network"). In a conventional fight, an army can directly measure their performance by the number of successful attacks against the enemy or the number of tanks or aircraft damaged or destroyed during a battle. Measures of effectiveness are difficult to determine and collect in a counterinsurgency environment, as the systems we are affecting are likely foreign to us.

It is remarkably difficult to directly measure the safety and security in a population and how do we measure the trust and respect between the indigenous population and the FSF? We have determined a few asymmetrical measures and indicators, however which may seem paradoxical. Such as:

The number of children playing soccer in the streets

The number of people who wave at or shake hands with the FSF during a foot patrol

The number of shops open during the day and or the hours shops are open during the day

The number of "tips" that result in a positive security operation (a raid, a weapons cache discovered, a warranted arrest)

The number of gunfire incidents reported in a 24 hour period

The number of effective IED strikes

The number of patrols in an area

The ratio of discovered and cleared IEDs vs. the IEDs which detonate

The number of intelligence tips which lead to weapons caches or warranted arrests

The number of street vendors selling items at a black market profit

The turnout of registered voters

The number of broken windows in public buildings

The number of potholes on major roads

The time to respond to a house fire

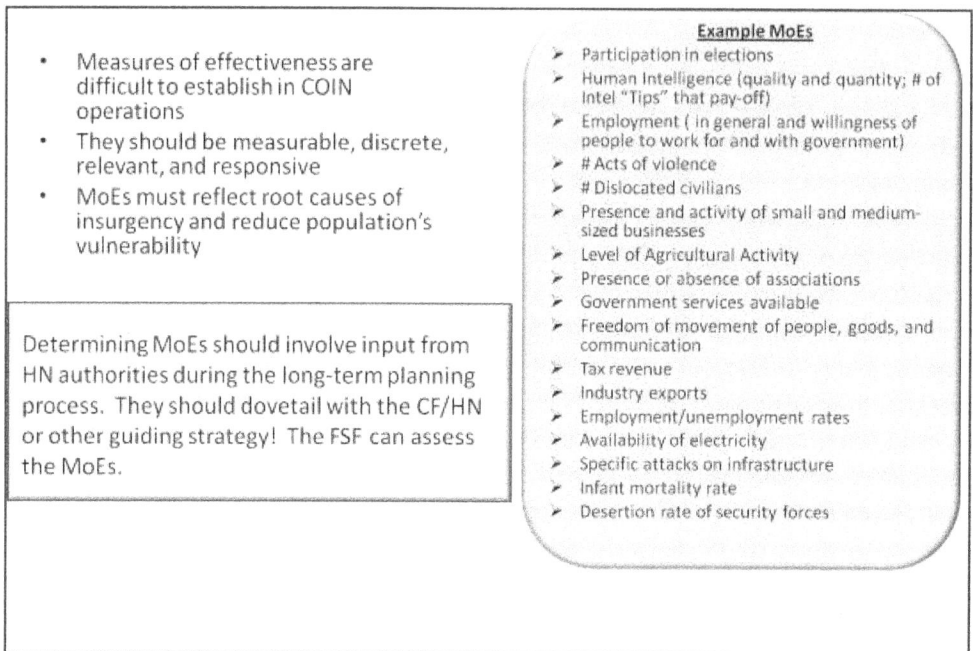

	Example MoEs
• Measures of effectiveness are difficult to establish in COIN operations • They should be measurable, discrete, relevant, and responsive • MoEs must reflect root causes of insurgency and reduce population's vulnerability	➤ Participation in elections ➤ Human Intelligence (quality and quantity; # of Intel "Tips" that pay-off) ➤ Employment (in general and willingness of people to work for and with government) ➤ # Acts of violence ➤ # Dislocated civilians ➤ Presence and activity of small and medium-sized businesses ➤ Level of Agricultural Activity ➤ Presence or absence of associations ➤ Government services available ➤ Freedom of movement of people, goods, and communication ➤ Tax revenue ➤ Industry exports ➤ Employment/unemployment rates ➤ Availability of electricity ➤ Specific attacks on infrastructure ➤ Infant mortality rate ➤ Desertion rate of security forces
Determining MoEs should involve input from HN authorities during the long-term planning process. They should dovetail with the CF/HN or other guiding strategy! The FSF can assess the MoEs.	

Figure 7. Gauge true success of operations with MoEs. They should reflect the root cause of the insurgency in a counterinsurgency environment.

The measurements listed in figure 7 illustrate more than the complexity of the question but also the quality of the target audience. Who are we focusing our efforts on? Are we looking to have a measured effect on the enemy/insurgent forces or the general civilian populations? Success in just one dimension does not necessarily translate to all targets. Therefore, we have to look deeper than one-dimensional effects.

Our partner unit, Task Force 2-7 Infantry, identified this problem early on based on the multiple combat and counterinsurgency deployments of their leaders. The US task force commander measures success for this tactical problem in terms of the mission, the enemy force, the time we are here, the general terrain in the area, the troops we are working with (ISF and US), and the civilian population (METT-TC):

Mission: What are we doing? What is our mission statement?

Enemy: Who impedes our success through active or passive subversion? What do we want them to look like at the end of our tour?

Time: When are we actively conducting activities in the area? What are the key dates culturally, militarily, and transitionally?

Terrain: Where are we working? Where are the areas that are critical to control?

Troops: What does the ISF look like at the end of this operation? How do we see ourselves? What units are on our Team to work with, including our enabler supports and interagency partners?

Civilians: What are the most crucial things affecting the civilian population in this operation? How do we want to improve their condition by the end of this operation? What are our priorities for effort?

Figure 8. 17th Iraqi Army Soldiers discover and clear a weapons cache based on a local tip. These cache finds disrupt violent extremist network activities, prevent attacks, and reduce offensive capacity. The continued success of the IA fosters legitimacy of ISF capabilities in the region and US forces.

By understanding our tactical problems to solve and by using these factors, we can determine a set of priorities for our limited resources and apply them where they will have the most significant and positive effect on our target population. Simply, we seek to apply limited resources against multiple areas, generating multi-dimensional success.

"There is a set of scissors for every beard. It makes no sense to use big scissors for a short beard, you will cut yourself."
The general's comment indicating the importance of using a discriminating focused response and the perils of overreaction.

For example, when we asked the general, "How do you measure success" he began to discuss the perks associated with being an officer during Saddam's regime and today. I thought he misunderstood the question or at least was dodging it but we did not interrupt. Our US task force commander and our S-TT listened to him.

"In 1985, each officer serving in the Army was given 600 meters of land in the area to build. Land was valuable, even at that time but it that wasn't all you received," the general began. "We had stores for furniture and carpets and supplies for a house too, which we could shop in. Because we were officers, we could build on the 600 meters of land and outfit it from the stores. We could make small payments over 25 years in order to pay off the purchases. This built stability and job security and we weren't going anywhere."

The general continued, "Today, after years of war, we are seeing the return of some of these systems. We want them back to improve our professional force. However, the value of land and the cost to build on it prevents this from happening." The general paused, looking at us for recognition of his indirect point.

"So, are you suggesting that the value of homes is directly proportionate to stability?" I asked.

"Exactly," confirmed the general. "When the war began in 2003, people sold their homes for a few million Iraqi dinar [around $10,000, we later confirmed] and fled the country. Some unscrupulous people purchased these homes. Some criminals terrorized people out of their homes or just stole them. Now, seven years later, those homes legally purchased for $10,000 are selling for $600,000."

In summary, when security is absent, home prices are low to reflect fear and uncertainty. Now that stability has returned, the home values have stabilized and they are fair values.

Using this same analysis, the prices of staple foods such as milk, rice, eggs, and vegetables are inversely proportional to the security situation. The prices of food staples are high during times of crisis and low (or normalized) when relative stability returns. Accordingly, home prices may be difficult to track. However, a human terrain team, a local national interpreter, a civil affairs team, or any number of other folks can track the consumer prices of staple food items. We have adopted this procedure across the AAB based on the AAB commander's directive. Each week, we observe the relative stability of the area based on the enemy (number of attacks, their effectiveness, types of ordnance used in IEDs, etc) and the people (the price index of staple foods, the words on the street, etc).

Often, Iraqis do not offer direct answers to these tough questions. They use parables, maxims, and old sayings to explain things which we are left to interpret. These responses are not cryptic to our Iraqi counterparts but these responses can be tough for our western linear mentality to interpret.

For example, recently the US AAB commander was discussing some of the successes in the 17th IA Division with the general. "*Sadee*, the results from the Ministry of Defense inspection was a great victory for you. How do you handle that success?"

"Men enjoy fruit from the best trees," the general begins. "Of course in order to get the best fruit, you have to throw stones at the tree." The general puffed on his cigarette. "No one throws stones at a dead tree of course!"

We all laughed, as the translation finished. What the general implied was although inspection results appeared great on paper; some senior officers have some bitterness or jealousy as a result of such high marks. The division will accept the results of the inspection and weather the effects of that success. Such dialogue is impossible without developing a relationship built from mutual respect.

Section III

Advisors and Partners with FSF Counterparts

"Many partner, few advise."
Lieutenant Colonel Dave Wood, Commander, 1-353rd Bn, 162nd Infantry Training Brigade, responsible for training and preparing advisors and AABs to fight alongside Foreign Security Forces in SFA missions.

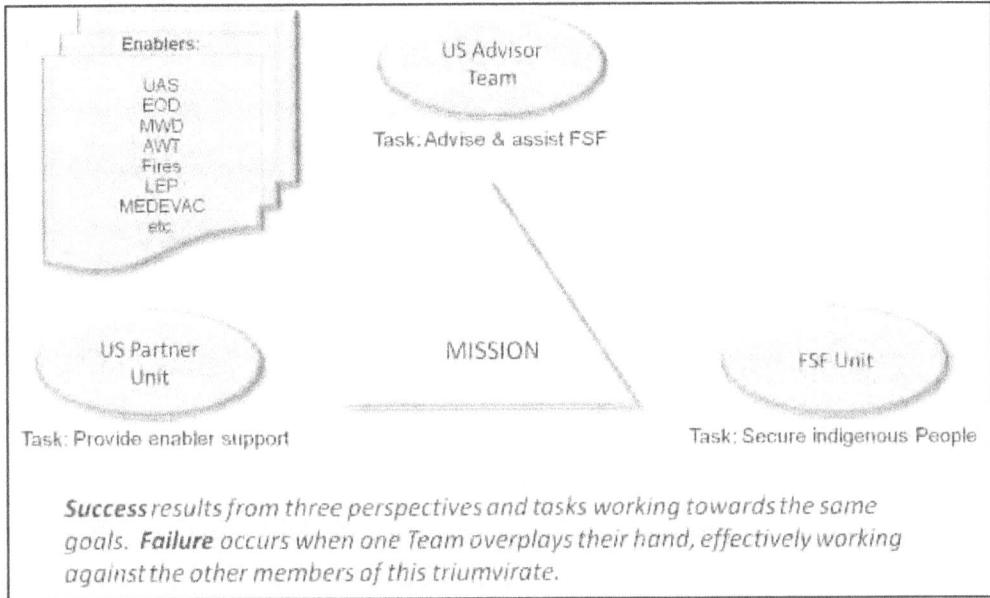

Figure 9. Triumvirate of Partner-Advisor-FSF Units.

In Security Force Assistance (SFA) missions, the roles of the partner units and advisor teams complement each other. Both provide enduring support to the Foreign Security Force (FSF) unit in the area. The degree of support provided is inversely proportional to the capacity of the FSF unit to sustain and operate on its own. In general, as the FSF increases their capabilities to secure their own population, the role of the US diminishes both for partnering and advising. Ultimately, the goal is for the FSF to stand alone, having built enduring relationships with the US forces they have worked and grown with. This is the disengagement strategy.

The 1/3 AAB had a unique operational problem to solve during this particular tour in Iraq. In short, 1/3 AAB was asked to assist six Iraqi divisions and three operational commands in the rural and urban Baghdad areas. The enemy forces we faced consisted of Sunni groups, Shia groups, and violent criminals, which were all vying for political consideration and power. This all had to be done while transitioning to State Department primacy, responsibly drawing down our forces, and transferring bases to Iraqi Security Force control. Further, the operating environment asked us to perform this complex series of missions while cultivating professional relationships for long term strategic partnership with our Iraqi counterparts. Yikes!

21

Figure 10. Advisor, AAB Commander and US Task Force Commander arrive for first combined leader engagement at the general's IA Division Headquarters (January 2010).

The overall task of a single US AAB (Advisor Brigade) taking over for three US BCTs (Brigade Combat Teams) in the country's heart was daunting but not insurmountable. It violated the doctrinal span of control as designed in FM 3-07.1, SFA but 1/3 AAB's commanders adjusted their organization and adopted a new mindset for this mission. In summary, they successfully demonstrated the versatility of the modular Brigade Combat Team concept by adding S-TTs and shifting into three distinct roles: partner, advisor, and augmenting forces. In order to accomplish this, the US Task Forces in the AAB would have to increase their span of control and accept risk as we thinned the lines around the country.

For our particular mission, the American task force commander explained the differences in advising, partnering, and augmenting forces based upon their relationship with the FSF counterpart unit and the functions each performed. This is simple to understand at a conceptual level and provided each member of the task force to understand their role with the 17th IA (Iraqi Army) Division. It also clarified to the IA leadership the roles and responsibilities of each of the US units they interacted with. One must understand and address this role from the beginning in order to establish the framework of a good relationship of professional trust and respect.

What the IA Commanders appreciated most in this type of a relationship was to understand their input into our decision-making criteria. We explained simply, "The IA commander's priorities matter to us as they help us focus where we should commit our limited assets and resources."

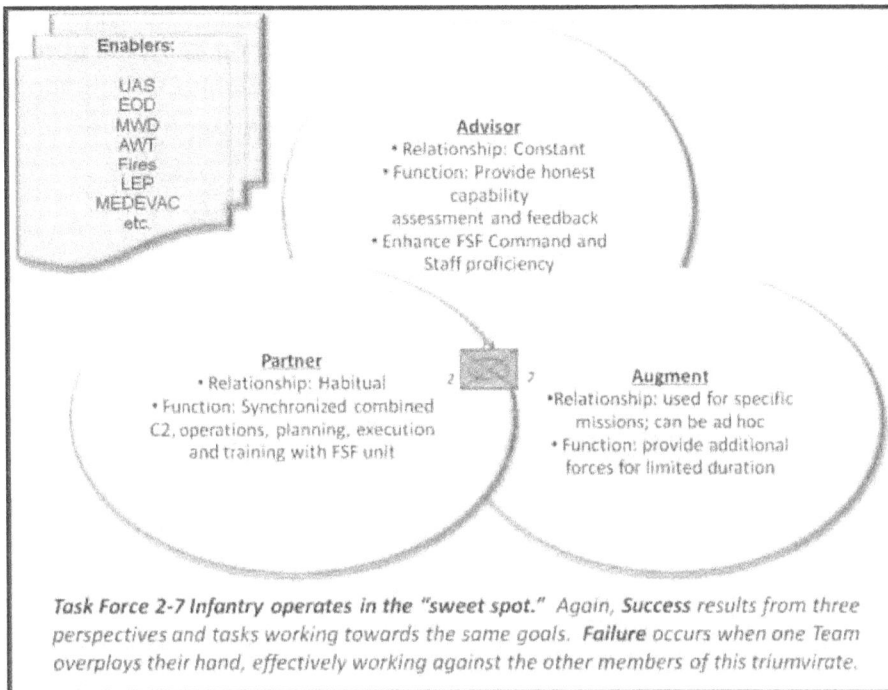

Figure 11. Role of Partner-Advisor-Augmenting forces.

For their part, the IA Commanders, when approached in this manner may be skeptical until we matched our words with our deeds. As advisors, we staved off this skepticism by immediately providing releasable intelligence reports in Arabic to the IA commanders as per their request. This was done almost immediately in order to establish good rapport and professional understanding that we have access to information and are willing, duty bound actually, to provide access to our intelligence systems and reports without reservation. This had an immediate and profound effect on the relationship between the US and IA forces in our area.

For example, the targeting process changed during our SFA mission. The US Task Force and US AAB no longer planned unilateral operations and by default, we considered every operation as a combined operation unless a specific reason precluded FSF involvement. We looked at the FSF commander's priorities and resources and the US commander's priorities and resources in order to develop a combined plan. When laid on the table, the general, the AAB commander, and the US Task force commander agreed upon a set of targeting priorities and understood what they could expect from each other in order to attack the targets, using lethal and non-lethal operations.

The resulting targeting process took weeks to refine and several three-week cycles to figure out what worked best for our units. It was the advisors who tied the process and ensured that the ISF adhered to the agreements too. The end result however, was a more efficient model to aggressively attack the violent extremist networks (terrorist and criminal) which destabilized the population. The US provided deep intelligence, access to systems, and advisors and small partner units to conduct combined operations while the IA provided the leadership and vast bulk of the ground combat forces as well as the ground reconnaissance and means to measure the effectiveness of our combined operations.

Figure 12. The general, AAB Commander, US TF Commander and Advisor (background) depart following the first combined leader engagement. The relationship was built immediately on mutual respect and a clear understanding of our combined responsibilities (January 2010).

Of course, the US side often times over-planned such operations as we are gluttons for organizational punishment. Accordingly, the US task force generated a schematic diagram for how we assess, coordinate, and synchronize operations between the US partners, US advisors, and 17th IA Division. This was particularly interesting to our IA counterparts who were surprised at how we took the guidance provided from our commander's intent and vision and generated operations along specific lines of effort. Everyone knew his role and progressed without over coordinating events, as a result. Further, a single slide graphic can illustrate a CONOP (concept of the operation) based off the same task and purpose of other operations. While maintaining operational security, this streamlined the process for military orders and resulted in a quick approval for combined operations and a higher confidence that a mission would succeed.

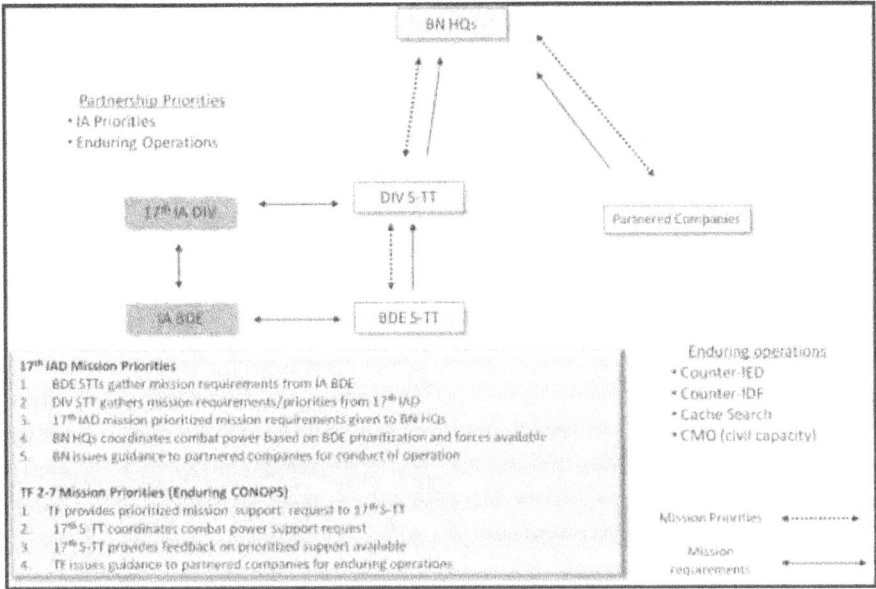

Figure 13. Targeting Objective Prioritization. Note the input of the FSF and integration of the S-TTs into the US partner unit process.

As an example, the 17th Iraqi Army secured more than six million people during the *Arba'een*, pilgrimage in which people go to the city of Karbala in Iraq and march along a road for 30 kilometers through the heart of Mahmudiyah Qada to Karbala to commemorate the death of the religious martyr Hussein. Commonly referred to as "the Triangle of Death" after years of violence, this operating environment (OE) stretched along the Baghdad belt. Accordingly, the US Task Force 2-7 Infantry supported and assisted the 17th Iraqi Army Division during the multi-day *Arba'een* pilgrimage which typically sparked sectarian tensions and violence from Sunni extremists against this high concentration of unarmed Shi'a civilians along the roads. The S-TTs were responsible for assisting the Iraqi planning efforts and rehearsals. Also, the S-TTs provided access to some US assets needed to promote a safe and secure environment to conduct this pilgrimage. The partnering American Task Force (TF 2-7 Infantry) provided five platoons of troops to run combined patrols and set-in ambushes and blocking positions. Additionally, they conducted combined disruption operations against several targets in the area, to keep the terrorist forces off balance. Simultaneously, the largest burden for internal security rested on the shoulders of the 17th IA who manned security weigh-stations and rest stops every 250 meters along the 30 kilometer stretch of road and more than a dozen sniper positions and 50 blocking positions to prevent mortar attacks against the pilgrims and over 300 vehicle checkpoints. As a result, from 28 January and 04 February, millions of Iraqi citizens passed safely through the area on their way to Karbala (about 70 km south of us) with remarkably no interruptions. As a testimony to success, Iraqi Commanders absolutely led the 2010 *Arba'een* security plan and executed with their *jundi* (soldiers) with US forces in an SFA role.

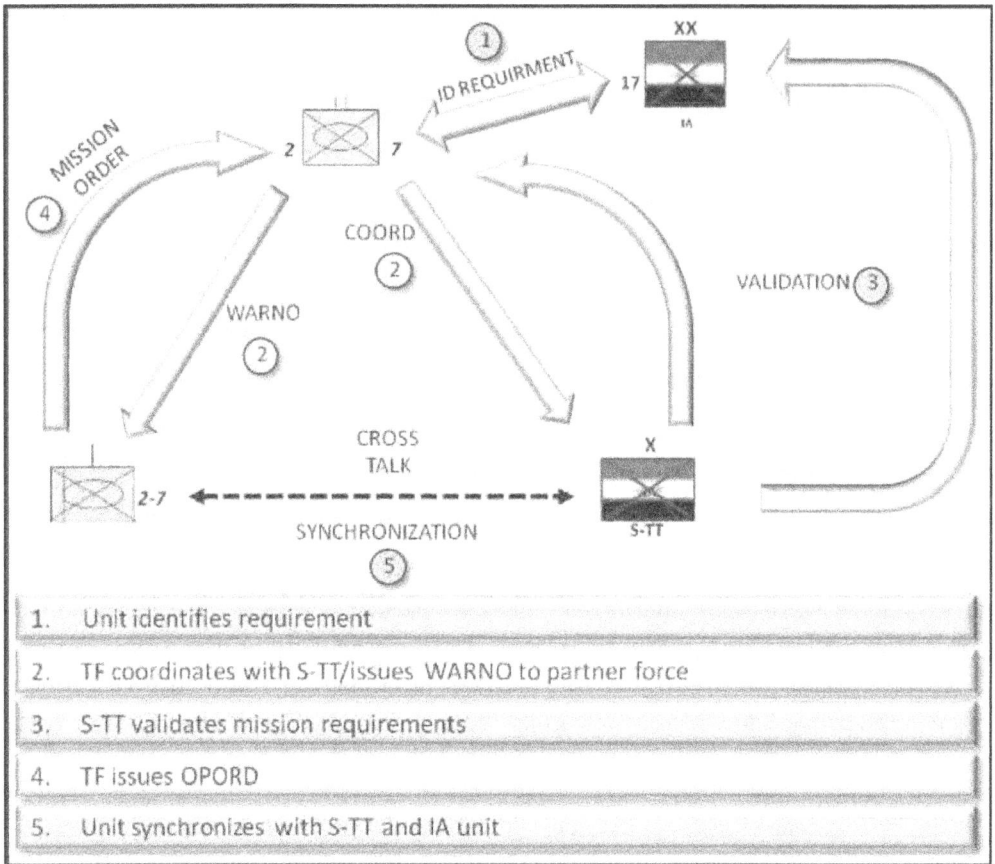

Figure 14. The process used for operational assessment, coordination and synchronization between US and FSF units. Note the S-TTs are the conduit for information - not decision-makers.

This *Arba'een* security plan illustrates the parts we all play between US advisors, US partner units, and the FSF counterparts. The design of our tasks and purposes met, complementing portions of the overall mission. Of course, it is not necessary to have a US partner unit when you are performing advisor functions but they certainly help. Having witnessed first hand the ad hoc debacle with our Army, confronted the call for military transition teams in 2005 and 2006. I submit my firsthand testimony that the AAB concept works when properly resourced and the right personalities are in play. Paragraph 2-60 of FM 3-07.1 states,

"Advisors are not partners…advising and partnering are complimentary but inherently different activities. Advising requires relationship building and candid discourse to influence and develop a professional security force. Partnering incorporates training with combined operations to achieve the same SFA goals. Advisors perform partnership shaping functions, shape discussions with their counterparts, and create opportunities for the partnering units."

Figure 15. Over 6.2 million Shi'a pilgrims safely travelled through Mahmudiyah Market in Southern Baghdad, Iraq during Arba'een (28 January and 04 February 2010).

This is exactly how we (the S-TTs and the US Task Force) approached our relationship with the general's unit. It worked brilliantly. To the point that on 07 March 2010, the general discussed the reasons behind the successful partnership with US AAB commander in the area during Iraq national elections. The general reported to his higher headquarters,

"We have seen an amazing change in relationship with the US Division, Brigade, Battalion, and Advisor Team. We are all on the same side...I consider us all part of one Unit. I am not just saying that because you [US AAB commander] are in the room either. It is clear across this division that the US forces are here to help us succeed. The people and the terrorists see it too. It's a strong bond and brotherhood."

The following day, the general continued his discourse for the reasons for success in the area and how pleased he was with the US advisor team specifically.

"In the past six years, I have had eight American advisors working with me," the general began. "What makes a good advisor is three things. He must be next to me, he must listen, and he must follow his words with action."

I nod my head in agreement, "So, how are we doing?" I ask referring to me and my Deputy S-TT Chief, Major Barry Horsey.

The general smiles, as he reveals our interim grade,

"My officers come to me, even though they do not have much (if any) direct contact with you, *Abu Damon*, and they tell me about you," the general continued, "I asked my officers how they look at you, and they tell me plainly. 'They are good and smart,' they say. I ask, 'How do you know this?' They say, 'because they are always with you and wherever you are, they are too. They listen to you when you talk. They answer your questions and when you are not around, *sadee* (sir). They come to each of us and follow up words with action.' (The general puffs on his cigarette as the translation is completed and concludes in English) This is why you are good advisors."

I firmly believe we are never as good as our annual Officer Evaluation Reports (OERs) profess but that was a ringing endorsement of how we are working together. A lot will be done and said about the effectiveness of military advisors but on this day in the general's office, we received validation for our training, sacrifices, and conduct.

Section IV

Good Advisors Listen and Great Advisors Learn and Apply

"Earn the right to be heard every day."
COG of National Training Center, Colonel Ted Martin, speaking on the challenging role of military advising.

As we embark on these Security Force Assistance (SFA) missions in the modern era, we must be humble and learn from our history. We were not always the greatest military power in the world. We began with an untamed fierce spirit. It was through discipline, training and diligence that we were able to conquer the greatest army of the day. The FSF we are working with today (such as the Iraqi Security Forces) are the only force capable to bring a sustainable security to the contested region. Only an indigenous force can secure its own people. We do not seek an American colony in the Middle East and only a friendly comrade and a neighbor with mutual respect. Treat every day, every patrol, and every engagement in this manner.

Figure 16. Iraqi Army troop stands guard as a professional Soldier in a force more than 500,000 strong.

We will not impose our will on the Iraqi Commanders and they are strong by themselves. It is our duty to advise and assist them in planning their operations. As a Brigade Combat Team augmented for SFA, we have a list of enablers to tap into and assistance we can provide, such as:

• Working dog teams • Database access (CIDNE, TIGRnet) • Scouts (GLDS, LRAS, recce) • Maps and imagery (plotters) • Situational awareness tracking (CPOF, BFT) • Specialized training (medical, TCP, patrolling, weapons, tactics, air reaction force, etc) • EOD for route clearance • UAV recce (Raven, Shadow, Predator)	• Static camera surveillance (for based defense and CIED over watch) • Night vision devices • Targeting cycles • CMO assistance • Biometric collection • Media outlet (Influence Engagement cell, TPT, PAO, etc) • Armed aerial recce • Armored QRF • CAS (Air Weapons Team) • Fires planning (artillery, mortars, illumination for C-IED)	• C-IED devices & TTPs • Operational planning (TLPs, MDMP, 7-step Combat Estimate) • Logistic sustainment • Class IV (wire, barriers) • Communications (CPOF, FM radios, cell phone, BFT, TIGR) • Detainee ops • Armed aerial recce • Law Enforcement Professional training (secure a scene, obtain a warrant, gather & process evidence, conduct an investigation)

Figure 17. A sample list of US enablers which can be used to augment FSF capabilities.

Encapsulated in this simple list of enablers, the advisor teams provide three things: *leadership, professionalism,* and *legitimacy*. Further, we should only provide the assistance requested by our counterparts but ensure the ISF understand what we are capable of providing as well as of our limitations. We assess the FSF request for support with their internal commitment to find a sustainable solution which means we must balance the FSF request against what they need to accomplish their mission and what they can do internally. Several times we have found that the cultural stigma prevents the FSF from requesting legitimate support.

For example, we observed a small IED explosion on a video surveillance camera near a crowded marketplace in April of 2010. We watched the response of the ISF and the local people in real time. The response was quick and decisive, treating one lightly wounded Iraqi Army *jenood* soldier because of rock fragments from the small homemade explosive IED that had lodged in his hand, while calming the people down and quickly restoring order. While the event was unfolding, we advised the Iraqi Officers tracking the event in the Combined Division Operations Center (CDOC).

"*Muqadim* (Lieutenant Colonel), your team appears to have restored immediate control of the area," we noted to the Operations Officer, whose duty it is to manage such emergencies and send additional resources to the unit in contact with the event or the enemy.

"*Na'am* (Yes)," he replied. "They reacted well but they must have been asleep to let an IED get planted so close to them. As you can see, the initial report, is that one *jenood* is wounded in his hand."

"So, what is the next step in your reaction drill?" we asked. Reaction drills to these types of events are routine in an operations center in the US military but they can be new to FSF who are used to the FSF Commander directing every action. The concept of a Division-level CDOC is catching on in the Iraqi Army and serves as a nerve center for tracking immediate events as well as planning future operations. As advisors, one duty is to reinforce reaction drills and conduct on-the-job training for the Operations Officers to react by a systemic drill to each event.

"I will go to the site," the Operations Officer began, "replace the *jenood* on duty with fresh *jenood* and start questioning them as to what happened. We will send the report to the Deputy Commanding General of the Division." Understanding that the evidence was currently still at the scene and had little chance of recovery and analysis with each passing minute, we wanted to impress upon the IA the need to secure the site and cordon the area so as to prevent disruption and minimize contamination of the evidence which could be used to capture the IED cell responsible for the bombing.

"May I suggest that you request the US Explosive Ordinance (EOD) Team for support?" I asked.

"No," the Operations Officer responded flatly. "The bomb has already exploded. Your team can do nothing for us but interrupt traffic." We understand the reluctance to request any assistance in the IA-led operational environment which Iraqis perceive as a sign of weakness or ineptitude. Accordingly, we had to demonstrate the utility of a combined response and the personal value of the enabler support in order to capture and bring the criminals and terrorists to justice. Knowing this particular officer, I determined an appraisal technique would work well.

"Actually, the US EOD has worked with your IA teams to show them how to conduct a post-blast analysis and how to gather evidence," we advised. "A combined response to such events like this is exactly what the general has asked for as well. I suggest we follow the general's orders together and see if we can gather some evidence to exploit the blast site. The report can be attached to your investigation to validate your conclusions and recommendations as well."

There was a pause and then, "That is an excellent suggestion" the Operations Officer stated. "We would be grateful for your help in capturing the IED cell. I will personally go and secure the site. Your EOD team can meet me there."

During this exchange, we were able to reinforce the IA commander's directives and how we should work through the FSF staff in order to make decisions that support the commander's intent. Sometimes an advisor has to apply slight pressure in order to ensure his counterpart requests the enabler assets in a timely manner and with realistic expectations. In reality, it took 30 minutes to get the US EOD team to the site and by that time the Operations Officer was already back in the CDOC conducting his preliminary investigation. The Iraqis gathered little evidence, as the scene was not secured from civilian foot and vehicle traffic but it was important to get the EOD teams into the response drill. The more interaction the IA and US EOD teams have at different sites, the better their relationship, the better the IA unilateral capacity, and the more sustainable solution when the US departs the country in the combat advisor capacity, and where these changes relegate the advisor to a lesser degree of activity and responsibility.

Of course not all advisors work directly with commanders. Primary FSF staff officers may require their own advisors or may share advisors across several sections. Examples may include advisors for FSF intelligence, operations, communications, personnel, logistics, transportations, engineers, fire support (mortars or artillery), media or influence centers. In Iraq and Afghanistan, we have used US Coast Guard, US Navy and US Air Force advisors to specifically work as small boat (riverine operations), naval vessel, aircraft pilot, and maintenance advisors. Also, special units such as counter-terrorist organizations, customs and immigration, border enforcement, and garrison support commands may require their own advisor teams. Staff advisors and technical advisors possess many of the same skill sets and staff advisors are the same species but a different breed. For our purposes, we will collectively identify these as "technical staff and special organization advisors".

The technical staff and special organization advisors follow the same principles as the commanders' advisors, however these advisors should focus more upon their particular area of expertise and how to improve staff functions in support of the FSF commander's objectives. These special advisors are normally part of a larger advisory effort or team but not always. They may exist for short duration missions in order to train the FSF on a particular system or piece of equipment. In any case, the principles of advising remain constant as identified in figure 8-8 from the Army's Field Manual FM 3-24.2:

Advising Principle	Description
By, With and Through	Not counting immediate action battle drill responses, the mark of an effective advisory effort is the amount of stake the Host Nation security forces take in their own operations.
Empathy Leads to Cultural Competence	Truly understanding other human beings and where they come from allows honest relationships to develop. These relationships are critical factors of success.
Success is Built on Personal Relationships	This relationship is likely to be tested on numerous occasions and challenges and only one built on a solid relationship of mutual trust can survive and ensure mission success.

Advisors are not 'Them'	Increasing the advisors' level of frustration is the rapid realization that, when dealing with partner units, advisors are not one of "them." The advisors are often alone navigating between two military systems and two cultures, never quite fitting in with either of them.
You Will Never Win … Nor Should You	The advisor attaining a tactical objective does not achieve success and we achieve success by the Host Nation forces achieving the objective.
Advisors are not Commanders	Advisors are not intended to lead Host Nation security forces in combat and they are ultimately responsible for command and control only of their own small team of US combat advisors.
Advisors are Honest Brokers	Advisors are advocates for the Host Nation security forces with partner units.
Living with Shades of Gray	Advisors will likely find themselves isolated with great autonomy, often with no supervision and will encounter moral and ethical dilemmas on a daily basis.
Talent is Everything but Understand Rank	The paradox lies in that some Host Nation security forces, recognized talent can take a back seat to rank. Advisors must understand that rank on the uniform is important to many armies but it is skin deep and the ways around rank are the relationship and talent.
Make Do	Advisors will never have everything they feel they need to succeed. Scrounging, bartering and horse-trading are daily activities of the combat advisor. An enormous amount of energy must be devoted to these activities. These efforts will not only help the advisor achieve mission success but also endear him to his counterpart.

As the SFA mission develops so must the use of American advisors. For example, the organization of Stability-Transition Teams (S-TTs) does not provide everything the previous Military Transition Teams (MiTTs) provided and S-TTs cannot cover the staff officers as the MiTTs did. We stopped covering the lower tactical units of ISF companies, battalions, and brigades. Rather, the S-TTs focused at the more senior tactical and operational command level of ISF divisions and area commands. For the 1st Brigade, 3rd Infantry Division, which partners and advises six Iraqi divisions in the country's capital, the S-TTs are further constrained. The doctrinal model of a US BCT covering one or two FSF Divisions was considered an easy mission compared to the daunting tasks facing 1/3 AAB. We transferred these tactical considerations down to the Functional Area Specialists (FAS) teams resourced at the Battalion/Task Force level which only provides limited assistance capacity and administrative support based on S-TT field grade officers directives.

This means that when the two-person S-TTs completely replaced the 11-person MiTTs, several things occurred:

- Reduced visibility of the FSF Brigade and below level

- Lower confidence in the Operational Readiness Assessment (ORA) validity

- Lower opportunities for partnership and the US partner units will engage with smaller forces (platoons instead of Battalions)

- Reduced capability to develop the FSF staff sections

- Increased reliance upon FSF systems for training and sustainment

- Increased coverage on the operation center at division-and-above level

- Sustained coverage of the FSF commander which reinforces the FSF command-centric systems

Some could have interpreted this shift in advisor-FSF counterpart as wholesale abandonment which would have been a nightmare if we failed to prepare our FSF counterparts for the reduced coverage. At all points, we talked to the general and his subordinate commanders and staff personnel. We informed them several months in advance and drew plans for how to maximize our remaining coverage in the prescribed time. It worked well and prepared our IA counterparts to manage their expectations without resenting the reduced coverage.

Figure 18. Iraqi National Police which are now called Federal Police, hold an internal meeting with US advisor in presence (2008).

As advisors and partners, our job is to engage with and not simply talk to FSF counterparts each day and provide advice and assistance. In order to have a positive and measured effect, we are responsible for forging a relationship based on professional respect and personal understanding of each other. This is impossible if we are ethnocentric in our approach. We must listen to their perspective and understand their systems in order to effectively advise.

That being said, military advisors are not indefinitely remaining on today's battlefields. Some have suggested the days of giving away "free chicken" are over as we reduce our presence in some of the most troubled places on Earth. As stated before, the FSF may ask for everything under the sun based upon the "man on the moon" principle and "You Americans can do anything. You put a man on the moon just because you wanted to see your country as the center of the world. You could solve this little problem if you wanted to."

These problems, best described as drivers of instability (DoI), are the specific challenges to the operating environment such as inter-tribal or communal struggles, sectarian behavior, external interference, violent extremist groups, or insufficient capacity from the legitimate government. When we peel back the layers of these problems, they are extensive, complex, and multi-echeloned.

Again, we return to the question of FSF commander's priorities, our finite resources, and engaging sustainable solutions. We should absolutely assist the FSF commander's priorities if it is legal, moral, within our capacity, and affects a driver of instability. Further, true success is developing a sustainable system which the FSF can continue after we move on. Our measures of effectiveness are those which improve the FSF systems and perception from the indigenous population.

Also, when this hard fought relationship is genuine, it is formidable to the enemy forces. They see how tight the bonds are between the advisors, the partners, and the FSF units and together they are a dangerous force.

For example, as we traveled through the streets of Baghdad, the general turned to me, "*Abu* Damon (father of Damon), you told me you were here before, correct?"

"*Na'am, sadee*," I replied. "My previous team worked in this area almost three years ago and during the bad days" (the 'bad days' are the common term for the sectarian violence which threatened to rip apart the nation of Iraq after the Golden Shrine was bombed in February 2006).

"You told me about a family you helped in this area, didn't you?" the general continued.

"*Na'am, sadee*," I responded, surprised that he remembered the discussion we had. "A little girl was playing in a field next to her house just up the road in the Abuethia area. In 2005, she was struck by a mortar round from Al Qaeda in Iraq (AQI) insurgents. She took some shrapnel in her tummy and the US forces in the area took her to the hospital and took care of her. When my advisor team arrived we adopted the family and paid routine visits to her and her family. We provided humanitarian packages of food, clothing, and toys for her and her brothers. The little girl, Amel, was six years old and terrified of Soldiers either Iraqi or US but her family was very grateful for the assistance and medical aid. We cared for her for the entire year and passed Amel's family to the advisor team who replaced us."

The general listened patiently while I continued, "We never cultivated the relationship for any human intelligence or anything and the family was desperately poor and used to serve us tea in a single cup. We would pass the cup around and everyone took a sip while our medic took care of Amel and provided medicine. It's all they had when we first arrived."

"If you remember the house, we could stop to say hello," he suggested.

I was very pleased and pointed out the house as we approached it.

The gate was close to a reinforced Iraqi Army checkpoint and we must have been a sight when we stopped and the general's PSD included about 60 dismounted Iraqi soldiers and 30 PKC machineguns.

Amel's brother answered the gate when we knocked and on recognizing me, the boy returned inside and got Amel (now aged 10) and her grandmother. We spoke for a few minutes and enjoyed the opportunity to look in on Amel who was now healed but remained skittish around Soldiers.

I introduced the general who seems less imposing around children, as most fathers are. After we spoke for a few minutes, the general surprised us all and pulled a substantial amount of money from his pocket and presented it to Amel's grandmother as a gift for their family. With that simple gesture and action, the general demonstrated that not only does he listen to what we discuss but he understands how to get the most out of people who work around him. This was a lasting impression and generosity is common in the Iraqi culture. My advisor team was fortunate to witness several such acts over our time together.

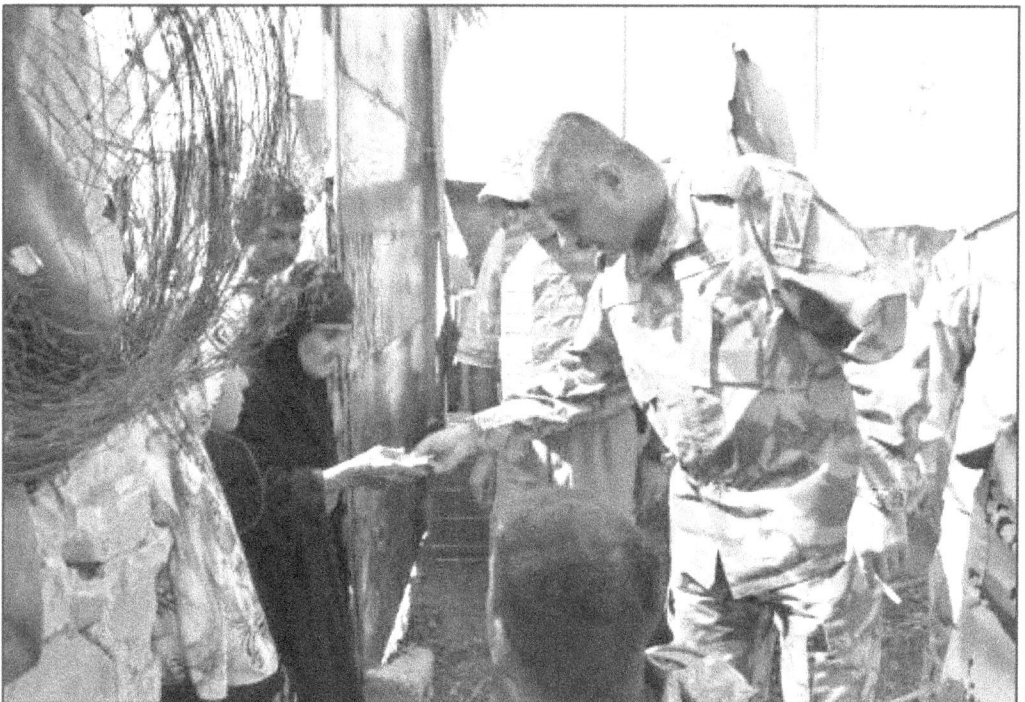

Figure 19. The general provides Humanitarian Assistance (HA) cash to Amel's family.

This was another opportunity to engage with each other on a personal level. I learned that the general listened to me as I listened to him. He absolutely understood that families such as this are often caught in the cross-fire of wars amongst the people. Moreover, the impact of advisors, partners, and our FSF counterparts serving and understanding each other on a personal level encourages our compliments on a professional level. One cannot learn this in a classroom environment and one has to experience this in order to understand it.

"We are writing the book on SFA...and putting it into practice. How are we gonna get after it [the SFA mission]?... We are going to attach our S-TTs to the Task Forces. The Task Force will partner with their counterpart units and the S-TTs will advise and assist...We will arrive at NTC 'ready to train'."
Colonel Roger Cloutier, Commander, 1-3 HBCT which was designated as the first AAB fully manned with more than 44 additional field grade officers who will comprise more than 22 Stability-Transition Teams

Figure 20. The general conducts a command inspection with a staff assessment for one of his IA Battalions in Arab Jabour.

Under Chapter 6, "Developing Host Nation Security Forces (HNSF)" of Field Manual 3-24, *Counterinsurgency Operations*, the train-the-trainer concept favored by von Steuben remains embedded in US Army doctrine. Since the US Army and Marine Corps published that watershed document in December of 2006, an open debate has electrified our military communities. The question was, should we maintain and increase our conventional weapons and tactics superiority or should we reconstitute our forces to fight the counterinsurgency fights that we are currently waging? Arguably, our institutional mindset has shifted away from conventional attack-and-defend tactics, which were at their zenith following the

1991-1992 Gulf War, and the apparent validation of Air Land Battle Doctrine (ALB). Full Spectrum Operations (FSO) subsequently replaced ALB in our current spectrum of conflict under FM 3-0 in 2008.

In FM 3-0, *Operations*, the Chief of Staff of the Army directed where we should place the emphasis by retaining conventional superiority while fighting asymmetrical threats and most sides agree that in the current fights, we recognize that the FSF are ultimately responsible for securing their indigenous population. Since the Army published the controversial FM 3-24 in 2006, several follow-up field manuals, training circulars, and joint publications have helped our military capture the battlefield observations of our advisor experience. The traditional expertise and doctrine from our US Special Forces community, who have conducted Foreign Internal Defense (FID) since their inception, primarily formed the essence of our US military advising. However, this is only one of seven primary missions conducted by the elite SF soldiers and the sheer volume of forces we required to build entire armies demanded that the conventional military adopt the lion's share of the responsibility for conducting these advisor missions.

تداول المقترحات الأمنية للمنطقة وطرحها
على سيادتكم من قبل شيوخ ووجهاء المنطقة

Figure 21. The Iraqi Army general, with embedded S-TTs, conducts a sheik's council

In the early era of recent advisors (2004-2006), the internal and external sourced Military Transition Teams (MiTTs) in Iraq and Embedded Training Teams (ETTs) in Afghanistan yielded some great experience. However, the untrained advisors largely figured out their duties as on-the-job-training (OJT). That shifted in 2006 when 1st Brigade of the 1st Infantry Division assumed the mantle of training the externally-sourced MiTTs and ETTs (including BTTs, NPTTs, MTRs, etc). This centralized and standardized the various training courses that other units followed bringing their course to about 60 days of small unit tactics and advisor training. Through the a 60-day training model at Fort Riley, Kansas, each year between 8,000 and 12,000 Soldiers, Sailors, and Airmen received some measure of ever improving advisor-focused training. United States Marines successfully transformed hundreds of their conventional USMC platoons into advisor teams through the Advisor Training Group (Shadow Team) at 29 Palms California by using much of the same immersion-style experiences. In the USMC 28-day model, the Fleet was responsible for organizing and training the basic combat skills so the reformed platoons could focus on cultural and advisor skills in the California sun. The crucial component of the US Army 1/1 BCT's training model was using former combat advisors as primary instructors and hiring Iraqi and Afghan civilians as contracted cultural advisors. This combination of direct experience and indigenous knowledge yielded great benefits to the future advisors. Also, the 1/1 BCT masterfully employed an outreach program, by which they learned (and taught) from other organizations the best practices for conventional military advising.

Figure 22. The Iraqi general inspects his *jundi* (Soldiers) at a traffic control point (TCP).

The 1/1 BCT training mission passed to the 162nd Infantry Training Brigade from Fort Polk, Louisiana in September of 2009. Now this organization has the primary responsibility to train the externally-sourced MiTTs as well as export their training package for the newly minted Brigade Combat Team and augmented for SFA (BCT-A) or AAB and improved the Ft Riley model to fit the shifting demands of the SFA around the services. In an interesting twist, the Army designated the 1st Brigade, 1st Infantry Division as an

AAB with a deployment window in the winter of 2010 and augmented with S-TT advisors trained at the 162nd ITB. The student becomes the master.

Due to the diligent efforts of several agencies, this advisor training is no longer without a firm doctrinal basis in the conventional military. In order to support their prescribed role, planners must take careful design in the organization and resourcing of military advisors either employed as a unit or as individuals. Currently, this responsibility to define the roles and responsibility of military advisors rests with the theater commanders in Iraq and Afghanistan. They have worked directly with the commander of US Central Command (CENTCOM) and the service chiefs to realize their vision for how these advisors will operate in their respective operational environment. Planners and advisors can readily find the roles and responsibilities for advisors and their parent organizations in Security Force Assistance (SFA), FM 3-07.1, dated May 2009.

Figure 23. The Iraqi general is conducting a command inspection of a battalion headquarters. Note that the US Advisors are in the background but not out of ear-shot.

The SFA manual is, as with much military doctrine, tough to decipher and universally frustrating. That does not preclude us from reading it from cover to cover as it's only about 100 pages and we must extract some crucial lessons as we prepare to conduct a SFA mission. Other short handbooks can also assist in generating the basic background for understanding the essential mindset shift necessary to earn the right to advise or partner with another FSF unit.

The SFA manual is the driving force behind the formal training for combat advisors to FSF. For example, the 162d Infantry Training Brigade sends mobile training teams to provide formal training in support of deploying units on:

- Language skills (Iraqi Arabic, Pashtu, or Dari)
- Islamic culture and regional history (Iraq or Afghanistan)
- Overview of the security forces and government (ISF/ANSF and GoI/GoA)
- Role of the advisor
- Negotiations and influence techniques
- Team dynamics and personality assessment
- Rapport building
- Warfighting functions staff review
- Preparing American advisors
- Counterinsurgency
- Stability operations and SFA
- Operational Readiness Assessment
- Leader engagements

Each Advise and Assist Brigade (AAB) may approach training advisors differently. Commanders may use ad hoc teams in favor of breaking up combat power or hybrid solutions to these complex challenges may arise. For 1/3 HBCT, the AAB commander and his staff quickly identified several operating maxims as we approached the 1/3 AAB concept:

- The AAB is a mindset shift in how we view ourselves, our partners, the environment, and the enemy
- The ISF are our battlespace and relationships are a "pacing item" which we track
- The entire brigade is organized to support the S-TTs
- Enabler support
- Training teams
- Staff assistance
- AABs are uniquely organized to meet environmental requirements and AABs will not look the same across the board
- As the focus shifts from brigades to divisions, S-TT task organization will change to fit emerging need
- AABs must see the ISF better than they see themselves and we are an observer/controller or OC-like network that actively participates with the ISF
- Agile Battle Command through combined operations centers are a way to both train the Iraqi staff as well as maintain situational awareness as less US forces are out in the operational environment

"AAB' is a verb and not a noun…We have to shift our organization fluidly and adjust it to suit our environment."
Colonel Roger Cloutier, Commander, 1/3 AAB

This guidance on mindset shift does not occur overnight. It is a deliberate process which requires specific training and detailed planning. This training plan, designed in partnership with 162d ITB, included four phases of training (A-D) which for the most part left the S-TTs with the job of filling in the blanks as to how to conduct the training. After all, the S-TTs consisted of field grade officers, who are brought into the organic BCT for a specific function and to serve as the principal advisors to their Iraqi commanders and senior staff. This is not a typical mission given to a Heavy Brigade Combat Team saying, "What the Hell do we know about how to train these senior leaders to be advisors?"

Accordingly, some of the S-TTs arrived early and worked with the 1/3 BCT and 162d ITB to put together a training program designed to suit the bulk of the advisors as they flowed into the team.

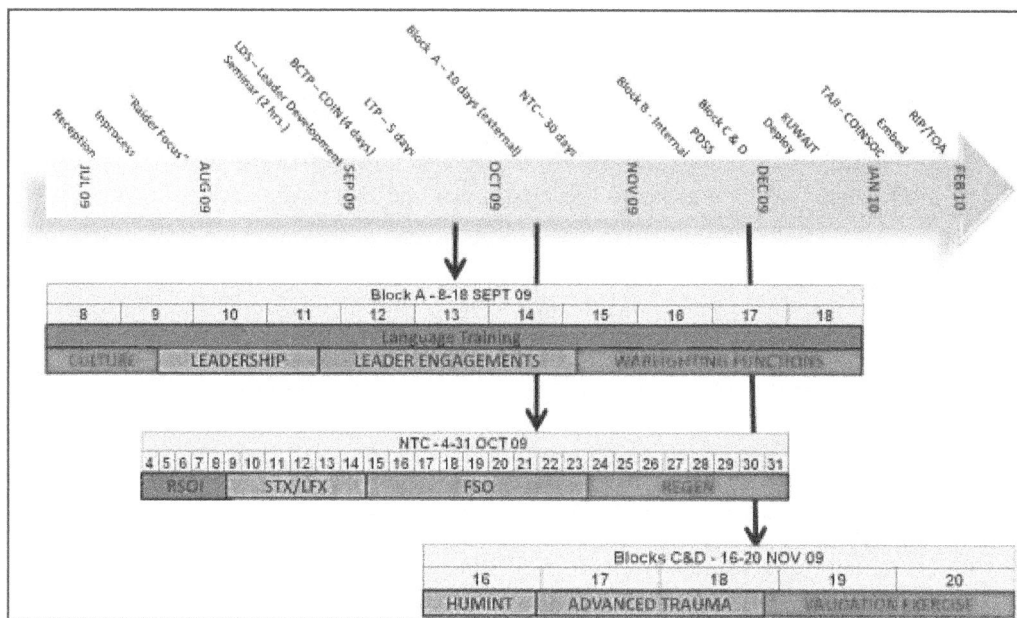

Figure 24. 1/3 AAB Training plan for S-TT integration.

The 1/3 BCT attributed the success of their training program to several key factors. First, early arrival of STTs is critical in order to allow them to participate in "Raider Focus" (the 24-day pre-NTC field training exercise) and gain an understanding of the brigade. The personalities matter in the coming fight and the S-TTs had to learn the Brigade organization and how they operated. Further, the early arriving S-TTs were integral in the development of the AAB architecture and they assisted the brigade S1 and S3 personnel and planning recommending task organization shifts to the brigade commander. Ultimately, 1/3 AAB went into Iraq with a similar task organization as they trained with and the pre-deployment training helped the BCT determine where the personalities and capabilities of the S-TTs and Task Forces matched best. Ultimately, this generated teams of advisors and supporting Task Forces who complimented each other for the benefit of improving the professional Iraqi Security Force.

To this end, all units are required to go through a Combined Training Center (CTC) rotation to validate their warfighting capacity within 90 days of deploying. This CTC rotation may occur at the National Training Center (NTC) in Fort Irwin, CA, the Joint Readiness Training Center (JRTC) in Fort Polk, LA, or the Joint Mission Readiness Center (JMRC) in Germany. These CTC rotations are improving their support to such AAB missions while ensuring the deploying Soldiers can fight in accordance with the rules of engagement. The 1/3 AAB validated their task organization during this CTC rotation which provided 21 partnered organizations and met the 1/3 AAB training objectives. Following the CTC rotation, we captured some of the most significant lessons learned to integrate the S-TTs into the AABs and how to prepare the unit for an advise and assist mission.

S-TT Integration for Combined Training Center (CTC) rotations

Below is a series of open suggestions of how 1/3 BCT prepared for an advisor-focused training rotation at a CTC prior to conducting a Security Force Assistance mission as 1/3 AAB.

Planning Phase

- **Early integration.** Attach S-TTs to Battalion Task Forces prior to NTC planning. This will assist with everything from clarity of BN/TF commander's intent through the capabilities of the S-TTs and how the partnering and advising relationship should work.

- **Identify composition of Stability and Transition Team (S-TT).** A S-TT is not simply two field grade officers. From FM 3-07.01, *Security Force Assistance*, the two FGOs are called the Augmented Advisors (AAs). Other elements of the S-TT are the FAS and the Support Platoon (SPT). The SPT Platoon is primarily responsible for the force protection of the entire S-TT and to set the example for the FSF to follow. They are the tactical arm of the S-TT. Another element of the S-TT is the Functional Area Specialists (FAS). This is, of course, dependent on resources.

- **Command and Control relationships.** There are several C2 models which have been attempted. Due to the large scope of the Foreign Security Forces (FSF) supplemented by up to 24 S-TTs (1/3 BCT used 21 teams during this CTC rotation), which will ultimately fall-in on six Iraqi Security Force (ISF) Divisions in Baghdad, the Brigade Commander realized that he could not positively control 24 additional platoons, each led by a colonel or lieutenant colonel. Thus, we opted to attach each of the S-TTs to a BN/TF. Subsequently, each of the Division-level S-TTs would have a Company in direct support of the S-TT.

- During planning (prior to LTP) the BCT must identify to the CTC how many S-TTs they intend on bringing. They should intend on brining their full compliment even if not all of the field grade officers (Augmented Advisors) will be physically present for the rotation. This will be a constraint for the CTC personnel and affect their request for role players and contracted support. Resources are finite and the earlier the CTC can support the request for training, the better the rotation will be. Further, the BN/TFs should replicate their support for the S-TTs and each team will have a Company Intelligence Support Team (CoIST), a maneuver platoon designated for support, and a team of Functional Area Specialists (FAS).

Leadership Training Program (LTP) at Ft Irwin.

- Planners can integrate the S-TT into the brigade operations order as a Foreign Security Forces (FSF) cell. This may not be an enduring capability for the brigade staff, however, the S-TT should simultaneously train brigade staff (such as PMO, CA and Fires Support officer) as well as staff primaries to consider the FSF in capabilities and operational status in their decision making and Course of Action (COA) Development. The FSF Cell is primarily responsible for understanding and briefing the FSF portion of "Military (M)" in PMESII and developing a concept of support for S-TT integration.

- As part of the FSF cell, the AAs should have some clearly delineated responsibilities in the operational planning process. See Annex B: planning Standing Operational Procedure (SOP) for Foreign Security Force Planning Cell for the ISF cell that we used during LTP at Fort Irwin.

- BN/TFs designate Support (SPT) platoon and Functional Area Specialist (FAS) team as part of final OPORD. Planners should describe in detail the concept of support down to key tasks.

- Between LTP and RSOI at NTC, the AAs clarify task and purpose of the S-TT which comprise the AA, FAS, and SPT elements. Further, AAs coordinate with BN/TF commanders in order to rehearse Key Leader Engagements (KLEs) and clearly identify their rules of KLE in order to alleviate confusion between the commanders of the partner unit and the advisors to the FSF unit. Failure to make this coordination can lead to misunderstandings and information fratricide between the AAs and BN/TFs.

Reception, Staging, Onward-forward, and Integration (RSOI) phase

- AAs should fly manifested to NTC with their BN/TFs. The BN/TFs would be the best solution in a perfect world but in reality, the HHC BDE has the assets and mechanisms to support the Defense Department travel forms DD 1610 and transportation of Augmented Advisors into the NTC. For example, the military orders for the AAs will likely send them "PCS (permanent) to Kuwait with TDY (temporary) en-route to training station" or "PCS to new home station". This can drive questions and challenges for each individual Soldier and the BN/TFs may not have the requisite expertise to solve these challenges. The BN/TF should provide each of the AAs individual weapons, PVS-14s, PEQ-15s, optics (ACOG and/or M68 close combat optic).

- BN/TF should provide each of the AAs with individual MILES equipment during RSOI week.

- AAs will integrate fully into the BN/TF planning process during RSOI if not before. When the AAs depart the Rotational Unit Bivouac Area (RUBA) on Ft Irwin, their Bn/TFs transport them into their Forward Operating Bases (FOBs).

Company/Platoon Situational Training Exercise (STX) Lanes

- During CO/PLT STX lanes, there are no clear tasks or training lanes for the AAs. Therefore, the AAs learned the TACSOP of the support platoons and accompanied them as "participating observers". In essence, the AAs conducted the STX lanes as riflemen in the platoon (allowing the platoon's leader and sergeant to lead everything to include the KLEs). Our job was to help guide the platoon leader and to familiarize ourselves with the PLTs TACSOP.

- Some successful BN/TFs integrated the AAs into the refined planning process.

- Though S-TTs have no clear training responsibilities or requirements, the initial relationship with the FSF commander and staff can begin. This initial rapport building session can quickly overwhelm the role players though, so take some time and spread out the meetings to just a couple per day such as one in morning and one in early evening which worked for us. We provided tours of our tactical operations center or TOC and some static displays of the weapons systems, LRAS, COLT, and other key pieces of ISR which helped highlight the US capabilities that we are bringing to the fight. An aerial reconnaissance flight can also be coordinated for this week or early in the FSO phase. This works well and resulted in a "quick win" for understanding the US-FSF relationships and capabilities.

- **Dedicated interpreters.** Each S-TT must have a dedicated interpreter either a skill indicator 09L or contractor. This is important from the very beginning of training and if the US forces or FSF counterparts have any issues with the interpreter, they can shuffle and resolve them prior to the Full-Spectrum Operations phase of training.

Command Post Exercise (CPX)

- Again, though none of the 207 injects directly pertained to or stressed the S-TTs, the AAs (if not out with their support platoons) can assist the BN/TF TOC to consider how to notify the FSF counterparts who share the same base camp and project some planning operations. Training centers can replicate the FSF role in our CPX through the AAs.

- **Combined Tactical Operations Center.** We immediately invited the FSF leadership and their staffs into our TOC. We provided them with a tour of our facilities and offered the FSF leadership computers and workspace. At their request, they received photo badges granting them unlimited access (English & Arabic) to the camp and TOC. They accepted the offer however they never actually occupied the chairs or desks. This is a role-player restriction, i.e. the role playing contractors didn't have their own TOC to work in. Regardless, we took that mentality of adopting Combined Operations Center when we ultimately arrived in Iraq (see figure 25).

- **FSF Commander's Intent.** As rapidly as advisors build rapport, they should attempt to extract the FSF Commander's priorities. These may change over time but they can help drive the initial targeting cycle. For example, one ISF brigade commander's priorities in one area included 1) Stop mortar & rocket attacks, 2) Stop smuggling of weapons and medicine, 3) Stop IEDs and VBIEDS, 4) Promote sustainable economic development in cities. Over time, the AAs and TF Commander were able to address the FSF commander's priorities during the targeting briefs in order to generate concurrence and to ensure we were focusing our efforts towards the same goals.

Figure 25. The general opens new CDOC for 17th IA Division.

- When the script ran out, we discovered that as AAs, we heavily engaged the FSF counterparts during the first week of training prior to FSO. The FSF role-players did not have a fully developed script to follow and were reticent to ad-lib in the absence of direct guidance. This was fine with the AAs, as we found the FSF role-players spent much of their time (when not decisively engaged with a counterpart) in their tent or around a table and often with the AAs discussing real world issues that were outside of the "NTC script". This was not just limited to the CPX phase but it began there. This actually worked well with the AAs during CPX, as they built genuine understanding of their FSF counterparts and how to best work together. Remember, the vast majority of the role players at NTC were not Iraqi and even fewer had formal military training or had been in Iraq since Operation Iraqi Freedom began in 2003 and the same can be said for Afghanistan.

Full-spectrum Operations (FSO)

- **Reporting.** S-TTs (now fully integrated into the BN/TF) should integrate their daily SITREPs into the BN/TF SITREPs. We initially attempted dual reporting chains through the S-TTs and discovered that we did not have enough communications assets to sustain a dual reporting chain. Dual reports and dual Battle Update Briefings (BUBs) caused competition for scarce resources such as CPOF terminals and SIPR. This only got worse over time when attempting to use limited terminals while planning parallel CONOPs and particularly when the FSF counterparts were present. Further, we initiated a S-TT daily read folder on the SIPR portal for the US BCT commander to read. This may be more beneficial in a down-range area where CPOF terminals and SIPR are plentiful in a mature theater but strained the NTC assets and caused friction between AAs and the BN/TFs who were all attempting to satisfy their reporting requirements. Further, this dual reporting contributed to redundant (at best) and incongruent (at worse) reporting sent to higher headquarters. The chain of command is clear. The BN/TF should integrate their attached S-TTs into a clear reporting chain.

- **Communications architecture.** This was a challenge, due to the seniority of the S-TTs and the lack of communications systems available and the poor reception from these limited systems.

- **Transparency.** We successfully opened our TOC fully to our FSF counterparts. There were no "US only" areas. This fostered an open dialogue with the FSF and permitted direct access of the FSF into the BN/TF S2's workspace.

- **Reconstitution of S-TTs.** During FSO, S-TTs share the risk and can be wounded or killed. We discovered a need to have a plan to fill S-TTs in case of serious casualty or fatality. Discuss this battle drill with the senior S-TT chiefs and the S1. We could cross-level S-TTs or pull a "float" from the BCT FSF Cell or BCT Staff or source internally from a company grade officer within the BN/TF. Whatever the decision and flow, it should be decided prior to FSO.

•   **FSF intelligence integration.** The FAS (CoIST) requires a dedicated interpreter to translate INTEL reports between the "tear lines." The S-TT provides these INTEL reports (translated into Arabic) and any associated warrants or photographs directly to the FSF unit S2 for his analysis. This will often generate a discussion where we can learn more about the report or from information not incorporated into the CIDNE database. This helps provide INTEL analysis and drives operations.

•   **FSF integration into Targeting Working Group.** As a general rule, the FSF do not conduct targeting cycles (lethal and non-lethal) like US Forces do. They have their own human intelligence of HUMINT-heavy methods of collection and little analysis conducted by trained staffs which generate their estimates and present them to the FSF commander. Our Targeting Working Group cycle is a way to improve the FSF systems. At the earliest opportunity, invite the FSF into the meetings and have the slides translated into Arabic for them (hint: when briefing the FSF, use less text and more pictures, it cuts the time required for translation and you can present them with a printed copy for them to take additional notes on).

•   **Warrant-Based Targeting.** The warrant-based targeting process maintains rule of law and FSF legitimacy in Iraq today. Prior to conducting an operation, FSF should secure a warrant from an investigating judge, as appropriate. This mirrors the role of the FSF used in theater today.

•   **Combined pre-briefs and de-briefs.** Prior to all patrols or operations, the Company Intel Support Team (CoIST) is responsible for briefing the departing force (US and FSF) on the latest intelligence and SIGACTs. Further, the leader of the patrol or operations needs to review Priority Intelligence Requirements (PIR) and the specific task and purpose of the mission. Conduct combined full-dress rehearsals not just a talk-through approach. Upon returning from the patrol or mission, take 20-30 minutes to get the FSF impressions prior to the US version. Again, the debrief is conducted by the CoIST.

•   **Combined operations planning.** A key part of advising is prevalent during the operational planning process. In short, the FSF may already have a notion of what they want to do and how to accomplish the mission or they may not. It is dependent on the FSF Commander, the strength of his staff, and the quality of information flowing into the FSF headquarters. As a general rule, by providing good refined analysis on Intelligence information, the FSF can socialize the CONOP. One example of a well conceived CONOP occurred about the third day of FSO on an out-of-sector mission involving multiple company-sized or greater objectives. The FSF commander, called to the division commander's headquarters, received a CONOP brief, and simultaneously, the US BCT sent down a warning order or WARNO with the general scheme of maneuver as negotiated with the FSF division headquarters. This permitted parallel planning efforts following our Troop Leading Procedures to begin. Upon returning from meeting with FSF division commander, the FSF brigade commander met with his staff and battalion commanders. No US Forces were permitted to attend. This generated an operational gap because every unilaterally planned operation (not combined) often resulted in time wasted negotiating and refining the plan. Later that night, the FSF commander requested to brief the S-TTs on the FSF plan. The AAs for all units involved in the plan listened to the FSF commander's concept which was briefed on a dry-erase board and were asked, "How can the US Forces assist us?" through our prior planning with the BN/TF, we were able to address concerns such as:

Present a Commanders' Timeline

ISR coverage, used to confirm template enemy positions (COLT, Predator, Shadow, etc)

Combined Rehearsals, to generate combined understanding of the concept and scheme of maneuver

Air Weapons Team, 2-4 x AH-64s on station designed to eliminate enemy positions

Close Air Support, A-10s, F-16s, F-15Es, and B-52s

JFO/COLT/JFAC/FIST, to control lethal fires

Weapons Intelligence Team (WIT), used to gather forensic evidence

Air Assault Force, 2-4 UH60s with US PLT to augment FSF unit

Suppression of Enemy Air Defense (SEAD) targeting for artillery, 2 x Paladin to soften

Route clearance teams, to clear ground routes (EOD, Compass Call, etc.)

Medical Team, 1 x Forward Area Surgical Team (FAST) can be pushed forward or augment Camp Medical facilities

Quick Reaction Force (QRF) or Reserve Force

Consequence Management Packages, lumber, food, water, tents, cots, other construction materials, and immediate financial compensation for rewards or to pay for collateral damage

Civil Affairs Team, used to support rapid atmospherics and assessment for follow-on projects

Media plan, 1 x PAO (S1) who can develop talking points, command messages, and themes

Information engagements with local civilians, 1 x Tactical Psyop Team who provide loudspeaker support on the objective (FSF Commander can communicate and negotiate with local people to get them to leave the area or move to safety) and assist development of products (wanted posters, rewards, tip cards, etc).

Figure 26. This raid was an example of an Advisor Support Team and enabled counter-terrorism operations we conducted with our Iraqi counterparts. It mirrors our training objectives which were validated during our NTC rotation in the previous year (October 2010).

In summary, the CTC rotation is an azimuth check to ensure the unit is on the right path to successfully providing advice and assistance as an SFA mission requires. Try some new things here and enjoy the rotation as it should look and feel different from any previous rotations you may have completed. (See Appendix B: Planning Standing Operational Procedure for Foreign Security Force Planning Cell).

For example, remember that advisors are not in charge which is often a bitter pill to swallow. An aggressive type-A Soldier may prefer to swallow a fistful of broken glass than work with a unit who does not have to take their advice or heed their counsel. This does not mean good Soldiers cannot be great advisors and rather *not all good Soldiers will make good advisors*.

Simultaneously, some great soldiers have a hard time adjusting their heads, hands, and hearts to the change of mission. One advisor recently laughed as he recalled a young Soldier commenting to him, "Sergeant, we came for combat and garrison broke-out!" This also goes to the risk averse mentality which some senior leaders approach SFA missions. You probably need to remember why you are paid for hazardous duty and qualify for tax exempt status - if your unit is more concerned with issuing blank adapters, boot shining kits and road guard vests on a Forward Operating Base (FOB). Combat has several faces, even battle-tracking with your FSF counterpart in the operations center or planning for a large scale operation is a chance to make a positive impression and maintain your warrior ethos in your approach.

Of course, these actions and activities only become lessons learned when we use them to change our behavior. This is where reading doctrine and applying it while conducting doctrine-based training and vignettes is crucial to developing our advisors. It is not enough to read a book or to conduct OJT as an advisor and imagine that what you learned or experienced is readily applicable anywhere. The tactical reality changes in this dynamic environment. Advisors must be humble and willing to listen to their counterparts. If advisors refuse this basic precept, they fail to learn how to apply their skills and knowledge into building a sustainable solution for their counterparts. Again, the advisors who refuse to listen and refuse to learn, quickly become obsolete.

For example, the general explained to us about the importance of the *sawah* or "Concerned Local Citizens" program in southern Baghdad. I personally viewed the *sawah* as a government authorized militia or paramilitary organization. I believed the *sawah* were not conducive for reinforcing the primacy of the Iraqi Army and police organizations. I believed the *sawah* detracted in a "zero-sum" manner from the trust of the people and either the people would look to the ISF or the militia for their security. Whoever provided security and essential services would earn the support of the people. Why are we authorizing these guys to carry guns?!

The general explained that the *sawah* are the people. They are all local and are going to defend their homes by their own hands. By empowering them to take arms and demonstrate a level of security and force, which is honorable, we co-opt their allegiance through inclusion in the security plan. The general ensures us that when we conduct battlefield circulation and TCP assessments; we stop at CLC TCPs too. He talks with the *sawah* and listens to their concerns and provides them with uniform items such as boots and socks as well as providing this to his own *jundi*. He does not have any other additional resources to care for the more than 5,000 *sawah* members who operate over 200 TCPs in the area but as a gracious host and compassionate leader, he offers what he has to the forces which provide security to the people.

Figure 27. The Iraqi general inspects *Sawah* (concerned local citizens or "Sons of Iraq") at an integrated checkpoint.

As an advisor, I was unconvinced of the utility or loyalty of the *sawah* until we began to speak with them directly. I recalled that the *sawah* were the core of the Sunni guerilla forces that we fought in past combat tours. It is tough to reconcile that these are now part of the solution to solving the puzzling "Triangle of Death." After talking with them at several TCPs at all hours of the day and night, we noticed a trend in their answers and the people and the IA treated them with respect for their contribution to security. Accordingly, their positions were considered honorable and their positions are not militia, who are considered as mercenaries loyal to a person or an ideology. (Note: the same is true with the *Arbakai* or Pashtun security forces in Afghanistan, who are considered an honored legitimate enforcement tool convened through a tribal council to enforce the decisions of a tribal *shura* or *jurga* council). As a result of coaching by the general and gaining firsthand knowledge of the utility of the *sawah*, I changed my mind and behavior toward the *sawah*. This understanding of the culture of respect and honor for the *sawah* has already paid dividends and the relationship also improved with the tribal sheiks, who are involved with all matters for the people in the south of Baghdad.

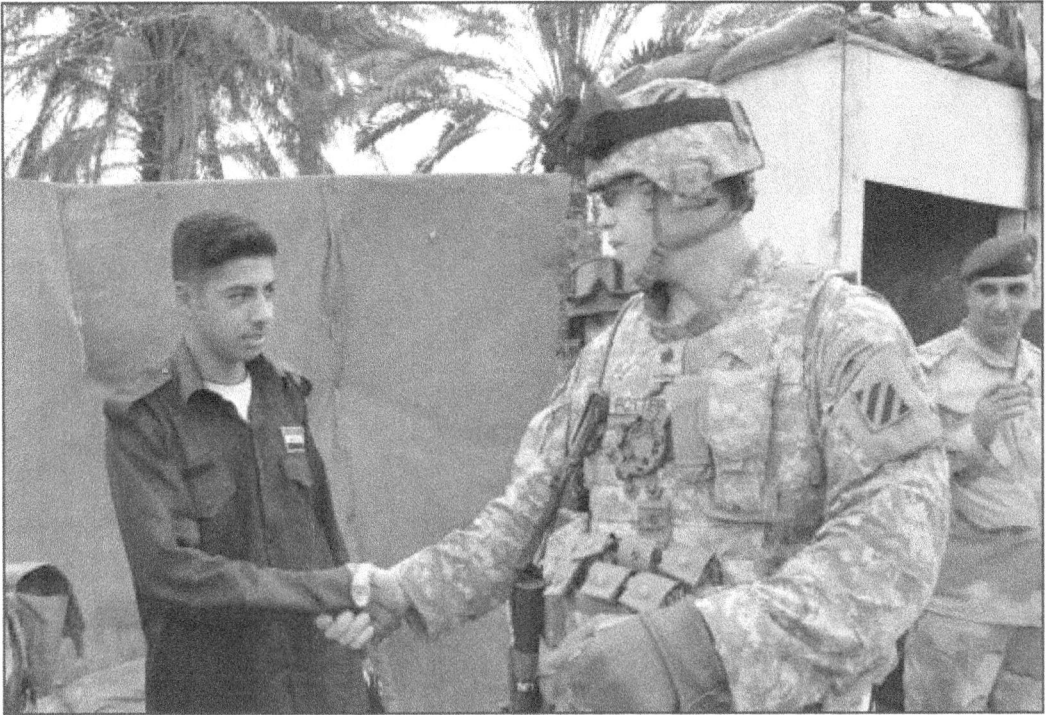

Figure 28. The advisor speaking with a young *sawah* (CLC member) who stands on a checkpoint, integrated with the Iraqi Army.

Ingrained in their personal and cultural values, the Foreign Security Forces (FSF) often will have their own ways of handling things. These are things we cannot change in a short one year long or less rotation working with their unit. For example, the Iraqi Army supply and sustainment system is a chaotic nightmare to a US logistician. Support is often built through "*wasta*" (personal clout) rather than filling legitimate requests for support or supplies. The top-driven approach to provide for their subordinate unit needs is rough to grasp for our American Army fellows. However, it is precisely this type of advice which the Iraqi Army rejects at its core and the sooner we understand this, the sooner we can move forward to filling the needs and other critical requirements which will help professionalize their standing Army.

- Advisors discover where to help a system and attack the challenge.

- Advisors discover where the FSF system needs improvement and the FSF improve, if willing.

- Advisors acknowledge where the FSF system can be improved and take no action where the FSF are unwilling or limited resources preclude our assistance.

This all ties into a system of rapport, influence, and control which is a delicate "mind-field" for the most experienced advisor.

Section V

Atypical Influence Techniques

"Listen to them and hear what they are telling you. You cannot learn everything from the last time you listened. God gave you two ears, two hands, and one mouth. So, listen every time to learn more. Then, turn what you learned into action. Let your deeds match your words."

Lieutenant Colonel Joshua Potter, opening comments when training advisors in Fort Riley, KS (2008)

US Army Field Manual (FM) 6-22, *Leadership*, contains several techniques used to influence other people (see figure 29). The 162d ITB exposes advisors to these techniques during their pre-mission training in order to prepare them to work with their FSF counterparts who respond differently to different TTPs. Understanding these TTPs are the backbone to advising, which is influencing your counterpart to adopt a TTP which is not necessarily something the FSF wants to do or perhaps does not understand the benefit from. We are not seeking ethno-centric solutions and such TTPs may force immediate compliance but are not likely to generate a true commitment by the FSF to adopt a new procedure or system. This is a delicate balance which one must base on rapport and personal relationships with the decision-makers. If the FSF decision-maker refuses to listen to you, then it's tough to advise him. Perhaps the best thing to do (at least initially) is to listen, rather than talk him through a challenge. The advisor should practice these influence techniques routinely in order to set a pattern of listening and working through challenges together and this builds commitment.

Pressure	Using explicit demands
Legitimate Request	Source of authority is basis for request
Exchange	A trade of desired actions or items
Personal appeal	Friendship or loyalty is basis for request
Collaboration	Assistance or resources are offered
Rational persuasion	Experienced expert provides evidence or logical arguments
Apprising	Explaining benefits of specific requested action (benefit not under advisor control)
Inspiration	Using strong emotion to build conviction
Participation	Involving others to establish "buy in"
Relationship building	Rapport and mutual trust are basis for request

Figure 29. US Army FM 6-22 described techniques to influence a counterpart.
Source: FM 6-22, *Leadership*

Understanding and using these influence techniques is an important part of advising. You must not only build rapport with your counterpart but use that rapport to provide advice, direction, and support to assist the professional development of the FSF. Simultaneously, simply understanding what is in the US military doctrine will not prepare you to perform adequately with your FSF counterpart. It is only your baseline of knowledge.

While conducting routine key leader engagements (KLEs) in Iraq, the advisors have learned additional techniques of how Iraqis influence each other in order to accomplish their missions.

Demonstration/ Intimidation	Open display of force (such as a heavy Personal Security Detail) which projects power, accompanied with leading questions or critical comments
Wasta (variant of 'Exchange' and Personal appeal')	Basis of personal clout and reciprocity, either real or perceived (Exchange and A trade of desired actions or items and Personal appeal and Friendship or loyalty is basis for request)
Shame (variant of 'Apprising' and 'Inspiration')	Demonstrate **negative** value for **not** supporting a position (Apprising and Explaining benefits of specific requested action and Inspiration and Using strong emotion to build conviction)
Deflection	Admit to limited culpability and attempt to shift focus onto new area of concentration and allows both parties to 'save-face' in potentially embarrassing situation and do not pursue or harshly criticize (demonstrate restraint of anger in face of contrition)
Restrict access	Respectfully deny meeting with counterpart and "the silent treatment"
End around	Go around your counterpart to accomplish an objective and seek information or support from alternative means in order to demonstrate resilience or reduce the perceived value of the personal and professional relationship
Wolfing	Over talking and interrupting is common during passionate exchanges

Figure 30. Real world techniques of how ISF interact with each other and their US counterparts.
Source: Advisor OJT in Iraq

These additional techniques balance real and perceived power with "*wasta*" which is a measure of personal clout between people. In order to gain *wasta* with someone, you do not necessarily have to provide support or a service to them. Some advisors believe that in order to get into their counterparts good graces, you must provide generators or fuel or food or water. This is not true. In fact, in several cases by readily providing such materiel support, the counterpart may perceive the advisor as a weak stooge who is ready to provide blind support in response to the whims of their counterpart. Worse, once that perception is established, it will stain the relationship perpetually and the advisor cannot retreat from that mantle of subordination. The advisor is considered weak if he constantly provides supplies and material items. Therefore, their best hope is to become a confederate of the counterpart rather than a respected ally (which is the goal).

For example, the general told me, "You could give me a room full of gold. That does not make you my friend." He picked up the coaster beneath his *chai* (tea) glass. "You could give me this coaster, if you have treated me with respect and it will become a cherished possession." His point was simple, if we are sincere in our attempt to improve the Iraqi unit, we will be honored guests. If we present gifts to the Iraqis without a solid relationship, there is no meaning or purpose. The Iraqis will spurn or squander those gifts.

Further these additional techniques help us shape who is dominant in the room of unfamiliar faces even if they have the same rank. The folks sitting closest to the head of the table possess more influence than those at the end of the table or lining the walls in a meeting. If a senior commander or sheik directly acknowledges you during a meeting, consider it an honor for it demonstrates you have maintained some measure of *wasta* with the senior commander or sheik. The same holds true if a senior commander asks you to walk next to him. It is not necessarily to speak in these situations. It is sufficient to listen and read body language. Always be gracious and direct with your counterpart.

Figure 31. US Advisor discusses training standards with Iraqi Army Soldiers.

Also, it is better to determine the personal values and professional resources of the counterpart before offering unfettered access to all manners of support and supplies. By listening to the FSF counterpart and developing a personal relationship early, the advisor can offer advice and assistance based on his counterpart's priorities rather than immediate support for all requests. This technique further allows the FSF systems to be exercised and resilient. If we, as US Forces, provided everything for the Iraqi Army, they would be dependent upon our systems and expect continuous support. By providing limited support in order to prevent critical mission failures, we force the Iraqis to use their own systems. This directly correlates to the operational level where we place our advisor teams.

Currently, in a paradigm shift, as the Iraqi Security Forces have dramatically improved their capacity, 2-person S-TTs are replacing 11-person MiTTs. This means that the 2-person S-TTs cannot hope to provide the level of direct staff and subordinate commander relationships. Rather, the S-TTs and their associated FAS will likely directly operate within the operation centers at brigade and higher levels while directly embedding with the Iraqi commanders. The S-TTs will be the direct link between the US partnering units and the FSF units. Further, they base their influence techniques upon the personal relationships developed with their FSF counterparts and appraised by their sincerity to supporting the FSF Commanders intent, balanced with their commitment to establishing a long term relationship with US Forces.

A challenge remains to understand how your counterpart exerts influence in his area. We can learn from their example if we listen, observe, and ask candid questions of our counterpart. Advisors build an ability to listen and exercise this type of influence over time and not overnight. Coming into the first few engagements and expecting your counterpart to adhere to your advice as law is ridiculous and particularly so on today's battlefields. However, once rapport is established and common understanding occurs, a small team of advisors can be tremendously helpful in maintaining situational awareness, building FSF capacity, and reducing the root causes of violence in the region. The measure of success is not measured by what actions US forces take; it is measured in the capacity of the ISF, and their relationship with the people.

For example, we recently discovered how the Iraqi Army played in the tribal justice system. In numerous incidents, a "*fawsil*" or tribal council is convened in lieu of the Central Criminal Court system of Iraq (CCCI). The process of convening a "*fawsil*" is contingent upon the appointing of a neutral third party to mediate the negotiation rather than pass judgment upon a particular matter. This process can take a few weeks but during the "*fawsil*" process, there is a ceasefire between the disputing parties and at the end of the "*fawsil*," the disputing parties cannot bring sanctions or actions against the other.

As indicated earlier, the Iraqi Security Forces commanders are sought for their neutrality in such tribal matters and often consult with the tribal power brokers. This system supports the rule of law in an area and is further outside the scope of the CCCI, although the tribal power extends to all key decisions in the area. This also reinforces the legitimacy of the ISF as a neutral force in tribal law.

The general stated, "I have been in this area for six years but never eat at a sheik's home unless it is part of an official duty. We meet with the sheiks often but we only have *chai* in their homes and never a meal. Why?" the general asks rhetorically. "If you accept a meal from a sheik, you run the risk of partiality. We cannot afford this. I know there are Iraqi commanders who disagree with me and they say, 'meals and gifts are simple tokens of appreciation.' No, they are wrong. By accepting these honors, we reduce our legitimacy. We risk our neutrality."

"We understand meals are a common part of your culture and solving problems," I replied. "So, how do you remain neutral and operate in accordance with your customs?"

"Simple," responded the general. "We host the sheiks on our compound and provide the meals on IA compounds. We cannot have peace in this area without the support of the people through the sheiks. Subtle factors such as taking meals together can jeopardize our relationship if it is improper."

A few days later, the general revived this subject during a briefing with his battalion and brigade commanders. The general opened the meeting by stating, "I remind you all of your duty to protect the people. We used to conduct two to three missions per day for each battalion area. Now, we are conducting two to three missions per week. This is not acceptable and we must resume our operations tempo as I refuse to believe the enemy is destroyed and they are watching us, choosing when and where to attack. For six years we have fought to reduce the enemy and not our activity levels."

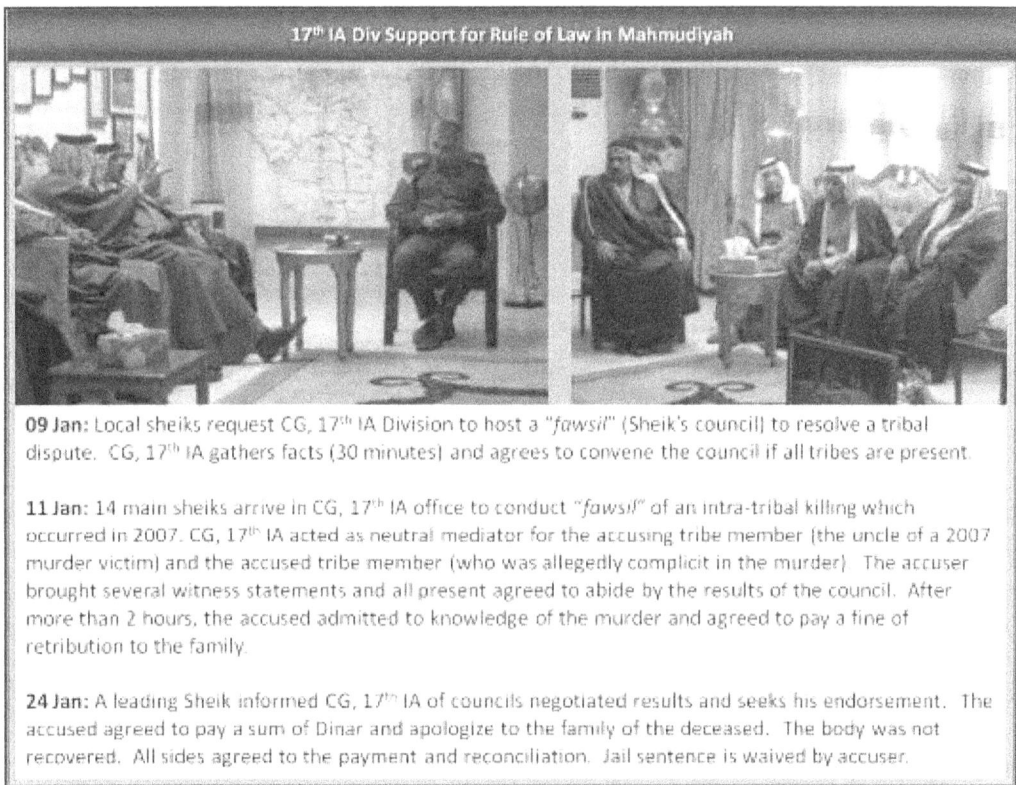

17th IA Div Support for Rule of Law in Mahmudiyah

09 Jan: Local sheiks request CG, 17th IA Division to host a "fawsil" (Sheik's council) to resolve a tribal dispute. CG, 17th IA gathers facts (30 minutes) and agrees to convene the council if all tribes are present.

11 Jan: 14 main sheiks arrive in CG, 17th IA office to conduct "fawsil" of an intra-tribal killing which occurred in 2007. CG, 17th IA acted as neutral mediator for the accusing tribe member (the uncle of a 2007 murder victim) and the accused tribe member (who was allegedly complicit in the murder). The accuser brought several witness statements and all present agreed to abide by the results of the council. After more than 2 hours, the accused admitted to knowledge of the murder and agreed to pay a fine of retribution to the family.

24 Jan: A leading Sheik informed CG, 17th IA of councils negotiated results and seeks his endorsement. The accused agreed to pay a sum of Dinar and apologize to the family of the deceased. The body was not recovered. All sides agreed to the payment and reconciliation. Jail sentence is waived by accuser.

Figure 32. An example of how 17th IA (Iraqi Army) Division supports rule of law through tribal engagements.

Later, the general reiterated to us (the advisor and the commander of the American task force), "This inactivity results from too friendly [of] relationships with the local people. Let's face it; some of our forces are asleep on duty. We cannot have this. So, we will change everything about how we operate…everything."

The general then went into details about how to initially reduce 10 percent of the traffic control points in his operating environment and use the residual force as a patrolling force in patrol bases for each battalion and over several months in the OE. The general desired to incrementally reduce over 300 TCPs to 50 percent reduction of approximately 150. This represented more than a re-allocation of combat power and this was a wholesale shift into an offensive mindset rather than maintaining a defensive posture which leads to complacency. The residual force should be a net gain of about 2,000 IA soldiers available for training, patrolling, and defending the national interests of Iraq rather than policing their internal population. Of course, the advisors and US task force commander applauded the general's decision and asked, "How can we help?"

This all tied back to how the general masterfully leveraged his relationship with the tribal sheiks in order to provide a secure environment for the people of Southern Baghdad. The design of his approach was to maximize his understanding of the area without subjugating his operations to the wisdom of the sheiks and he is, after all a professional military commander, loyal to the people of Iraq and not to his tribe or religious sect. This neutrality is paramount for effective command and control in such areas, not to mention essential for professional longevity.

Of course, issues of tribal law are not relegated to Iraq and we have witnessed several similar codes of tribal law and noted how the governmental security forces play into the system. Nor is the issue of using tribal security forces such as the *sawah* or "Concerned Local Citizens", an Iraqi solution to a complex problem.

For example, in Afghanistan a similar rule of law is evident through the *Arbakai* system. The *Arbakai* is born from *Pashtunwali*, the code of honor among the Pashtun tribes and however the concept has crossed into other tribes who have adopted the *Arbakai* concept. The system begins with a tribal dispute of grievance brought before a *jirga* (regional) or *shura* (local) tribal council. The tribal council solves the issue over a series of meetings and finally issues a judgment. At the same time the judgment is released, an *Arbakai* is established from all sides and neutral parties involved in the dispute with parity across the tribes under a single and temporary *Arbakai* commander. This *Arbakai* commander is appointed by the tribal council and is loyal to enforcing the judgment of the council. This force is not a militia which is loyal to an individual or an ideology and by contrast, the *Arbakai* are considered a legitimate tribal force where the central government has failed to provide adequate security in the rural, tribal, areas for a host of reasons.

Section VI

Perils of Advising

Advising is a rewarding military duty. However, pitfalls exist which can stain your ability to be effective. Through a combination of self awareness, training, and supervision, you can avoid several of these perils and serve with honor and distinction.

First, understand that military advisors operate in small teams (possibly ad hoc for the mission at hand) and are confronted with an inordinate amount of stress. Advisor teams often work away from their cultural norms and away from large military organization which provides internal support networks.

To illustrate the point, each person has a "snap threshold" in psychological response to high stress over time and multiple deployments, as is indicated in a recent study to explain why PTSD occurs and why it is important to build resiliency in our deploying force.

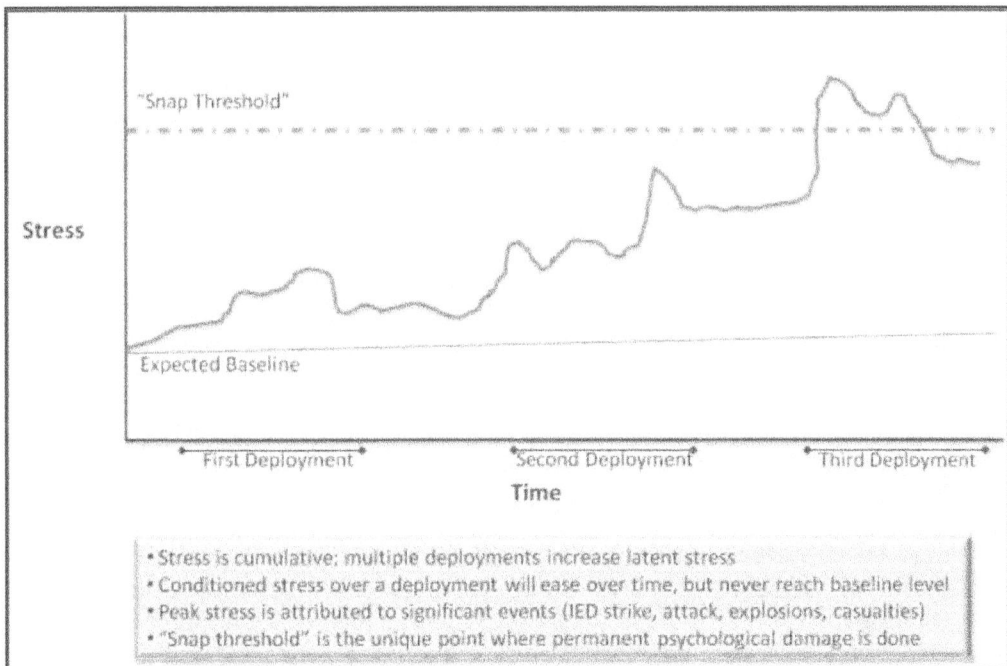

Figure 33. Stress over Time as a function of deployed experience, is directly related to stress of combat advisors.

The diagram in figure 32 further demonstrates that not surprisingly, stress is cumulative over several deployments in a combat zone. Now, take into consideration that American advisors operate with a foreign culture that they don't know and in a language they don't understand, away from the safety of massive US military formations. Throw in the ambiguity inherent in some advisor missions along with lack of direction or command influence, and you can readily see how advisors may reach their "snap threshold" quickly. The "snap threshold" is the unique point for each individual where permanent psychological damage occurs. It may be repairable over time and with counseling using such methods as cognitive behavior therapy. This helps explain why some advisors appear to have "gone native" or "simply snapped" and make degenerative decisions. Advisors require more guidance and course corrections from the chain of command, emphasizing their contributions, duties, and responsibilities. This will help them remain effective and in our nation's service for an extended period.

Another peril of improper advising is making minor mistakes serious by ignoring basic standards of discipline. These include lapses in soldier discipline such as not checking on your troops routinely or failing to adhere to a buddy-system, which can result in improper accountability in the event of a crisis response such as a mortar attack. Advisors must continuously reinforce simple base defense drills and the buddy-team mentality. The consequences of ignoring such rules can cause the perception of a "loose cannon" team which is untrustworthy and unreliable. This perception will degrade your reports of the FSF capabilities and subjectively taint your effectiveness as a team. Maintain the American standards of good order and discipline, as you will set the example for the FSF to follow in words and deeds.

Third, some advisors misunderstand "blame-shifting" as a personal attack or a challenge to their integrity. Referring to the way ISF influence each other and their US counterparts, blaming a problem onto a person is a common affair. FSF typically do not handle criticism any better than the US military would from a foreign army. The ISF in particular are often immediately defensive when a problem is exposed and blame whoever raised the issue. Most often, this does not constitute a direct challenge to the advisors integrity but could inflame a situation if the advisor does not handle it properly.

For example, the general told me, "I see our Division NCO Academy still has no roof. The previous unit promised us a roof over six months ago. Now they have left and we still cannot use the buildings for training because there is no roof."

"Well *sadee*, I cannot speak for what the previous unit did or failed to do." I responded as we walked by the buildings on his headquarters camp. "May I ask what the building will be used for?"

The general responded, "This is where we want to conduct all of our indoors training. It is only January now and it's rainy. When the heat comes, it will be 110-130 degrees during the day for weeks and months at a time. We need to have a place to train out of the sun's heat. These large buildings are it but, as I said, the Americans didn't finish the job. We have no roof. So, we have no indoor training area."

"Okay, what can you provide towards building the roof?"

"I only have people with time on their hands. No tools or materials." The general stopped and looked directly at me and addressed me in English, "The Americans said they would do it for us. You promised us. Now, you broke that promise."

I replied, "If this is a priority for you, I was unaware of it. We have been here for a few weeks now and this is the first time you brought it to my attention." The general bristled, as I continued. "Now that I know it is a concern to you, we can shift support away from another project and come to a solution now or we can wait until we can focus on it together." The general changed the subject to another matter and we walked away.

So, what did we learn? The roof clearly was a sore spot as it represented a broken promise from the Americans to the Iraqi Division. I later discovered that the reason the roof was not completed was due to shifting rules which meant we could no longer provide "brick and mortar" construction directly to the Iraqi Security Forces. The general knew this but it still didn't solve the problem. What to do?

Fortunately, our industrious advisor team had some excess scrap material from previous projects that were completed. Over the following few weeks, we gathered materials which could be used to repair and patch the existing roofs. It took time but we all got what we wanted.

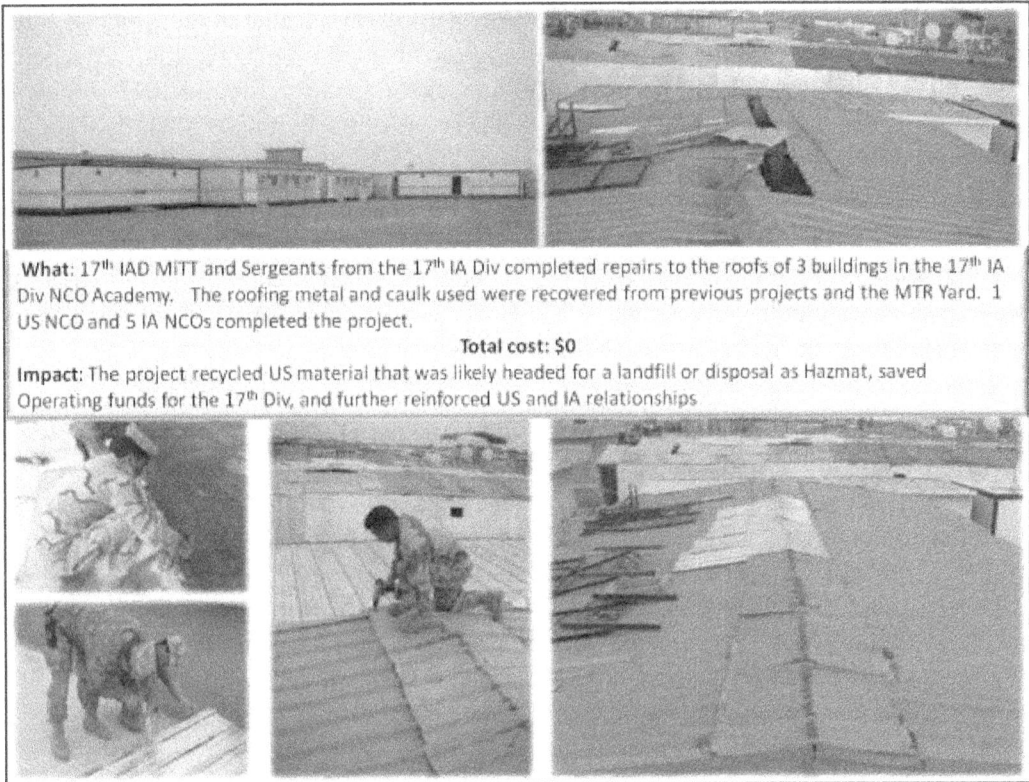

What: 17th IAD MiTT and Sergeants from the 17th IA Div completed repairs to the roofs of 3 buildings in the 17th IA Div NCO Academy. The roofing metal and caulk used were recovered from previous projects and the MTR Yard. 1 US NCO and 5 IA NCOs completed the project.

Total cost: $0

Impact: The project recycled US material that was likely headed for a landfill or disposal as Hazmat, saved Operating funds for the 17th Div, and further reinforced US and IA relationships

Figure 34. NCO Academy Roof Project.

Next, be wary of overselling yourself or your counterpart. You want the best for your counterpart because it will make you look good on assessment reports. For example, Operational Readiness Assessments (ORAs) had been used to measure the capacity of the ISF since 2005. The ORAs however, are not the advisor's report card. They are an objective look at the FSF unit through the advisors' access and lens. If advisors distort the true capabilities of an FSF unit, they may receive tasking to conduct operations outside of their capacity. Worse, if the FSF higher command believes the unit already possesses enough equipment, personnel, and material to accomplish a mission, they may redirect support to another ailing organization.

For example, a Transition Team working with the Iraqi National Police witnessed this in 2006. The Brigade NPTT chief routinely changed the ORAs submitted by subordinate battalion NPTTs by "marking them up". The report was considered inaccurate and unreliable because any US forces rolling through the checkpoints of the National Police unit could see they had low security standards and no support from their Iraqi chain of command. After six months, the brigade NPTT chief departed theater and others discovered the ORA embellishment. The US brigades and division which monitored the ORA level were shocked and surprised to see the accurate reports begin to flow. After the initial flurry of emails demanding, "How can this Iraqi unit possibly fall so fast and so low?!" we explained the misreporting from a senior US advisor. The battalion NPTTs dealt with the challenge and the tensions eased when they proved someone had earlier altered their reports. Our people fortunately caught the errors early enough to change some of the Iraqi leadership and send the entire Brigade to "re-bluing" training at Numanuiyah, Iraq in 2007. Today in 2010, that same troubled National Police Brigade is one of the best units in the MoI forces (re-named as the Federal Police).

Dealing with death can be a dangerous business as an advisor and particularly when the death is a FSF Soldier and not an American. The FSF counterpart expects the advisor to be respectful and listen rather than offer brief condolences and attempt to use the Soldiers' death as a learning point. Remember, all FSF will handle mortality uniquely. Our job as advisors is to be patient, observe, and help our partners and other US forces engage properly with the FSF following a tragic event.

Following an assassination of several Iraqi Army members at a traffic control point, the 17th IA Division responded quickly and heavily. They gathered more than 100 civilians from the area immediately surrounding the attacked TCP. Where, after questioning at the battalion headquarters, they released most of the civilians while detaining only eight. Some of these were recently released from prison and some had outstanding warrants for their arrest and some were simply unaccounted for at the time of the assassinations. After an exhaustive initial search of the area with a two kilometer sweep around the TCP, they discovered no leads after the first day. The general took our advisor team with him to witness the initial inquiry and to hear his guidance for action. Anger, sadness, tension, and revenge were in everyone's eyes as the commanders gathered to listen to the general's guidance about 15 hours after the attack.

After reviewing the timeline of what occurred as briefed by the IA brigade commander, the general stated these actions followed the same pattern from several months earlier when two other TCPs were similarly attacked. The common threads indicate the *jenood* or common soldiers were asleep on duty late at night, the attackers used silenced pistols, and the leadership had not checked on the TCP regularly at night.

The general levied a series of instructions to his commanders present:

Reiterating the signed agreement all of you down to platoon leaders signed less than five months ago at the division headquarters and all TCPs will have at least six personnel including minimum two on ground duty and two in the observation tower at all times, commander will check on TCPs at least three times each day and night.

Tighten security on all TCPs. Every vehicle will be searched at every checkpoint. This will cause delays and we understand.

Serve all outstanding warrants for arrest in your areas. Check with the S2s for a list and distribute them to the TCPs. Focus raids if we know where criminals sleep and we have a warrant for them.

Search all farms for weapons. Search all shops for contraband. Be respectful of personal possessions and the people. Respect the rights of females, children, and the elderly. However, make sure they understand that our Soldiers were killed and we expect cooperation to find those responsible.

Reward good information.

Be prepared to shuffle battlespace between battalions within 15 days.

Commandos will stay in the attacked battalion's sector to augment their forces and focus searches until further notice. You will dig around this place with a needle.

Prohibit sheiks from entering the brigade or battalion headquarters. You are not allowed to meet with them. There is no sheik higher than the law. If these sheiks are our friends and allies, they will come forward with information on the killers. If they come and ask for favors or a weapon permit or help on a relative who is detained, tell them 'We are busy finding the killers in the area. Unless you help us, we have no time for you.' The sheiks from the attacked brigade area are also prohibited from entering the 17th Division Headquarters until further notice.

All staff officers will check TCPs at night and do not allow them to sit in their offices or sleep.

Every battalion has assigned areas to focus on. Every battalion will turn up the heat and search hard. Find those responsible.

Respect those who cooperate. Remind the bad people who we are. We have been here since 2004. For one Soldier killed, beat back their head. It's the choice of the people now.

Our neighboring IA Division will hit an adjacent area tomorrow morning as a sign of solidarity. They share our loss and there must be no gaps between our units and no place for the killers to feel safe.

Detain the company commander and brigade S2 of the unit responsible. They failed to do their jobs. They will stay in detention until the killers are found. The new brigade S2 will come from the division G2 office and effective immediately, focus searching on individuals recently released from prison.

All Commanders will conduct day and night TCP assessments. If anyone is found asleep, the commander will be immediately detained.

If we cannot protect ourselves, how can we protect the people? That is what people will say if we fail to catch and punish the killers.

Remember this day as a memorial to our fallen Soldiers.

Cease planning other operations unless they pertain to finding these killers. The combined mission [with the US partner unit] scheduled for later this week is cancelled. Planning for the combined mission scheduled to occur next week, may still proceed.

Muqadem Potter, do you have anything to add?

So, with high tensions in the room, how does the advisor respond to this guidance? Be respectful, offer assistance, and listen. Remember, the loss of any Soldier is treated with the same reverence and professionalism. We are not in charge but stand ready to assist with requests for UAV observation, or attack helicopters as a show of force with ISR assets and military working dog teams augmenting the TCPs, etc. I failed to heed my own advice, however…

"*Na'am Sadee*," I began. My interpreter Jim cringed a little, hoping I would say nothing. "I am concerned with the *sawah* [CLC] leaders in the area. I believe they have TCPs in the same area and they are supposed to be on duty as well. They are also responsible for security in the area. Have we talked with them?"

The room full of Iraqi Commanders bustled at the suggestion and passed significant looks between each other.

The general, bless his heart, stopped me with a gesture. He reached up to his chin and gently stroked his imaginary beard. This is an Iraqi gesture which means 'slow down, demonstrate patience.' Recognizing the gesture I stopped speaking.

"The *sawah* are not to blame here." the general said evenly to his IA Commanders. Looking directly at me he said, "They are doing their job."

The meeting broke up shortly thereafter and I was grateful the general spoke to me privately in the car as we drove away from the meeting. "Remember were the *sawah* came from. Most had ties to violent Sunni groups here. If my IA commanders think it's okay to go after them, they will. We have fought long and hard for the *sawah* to stay out of the fighting. Today, they are on the sidelines and I do not want to give them an excuse to rejoin the fight on their former side."

The general saved our relationship and my credibility by politely telling me to shut up in the meeting. Another lesson I will not soon forget.

Another pitfall advisors must avoid is gently accepting "good enough" as a moral victory. Strive for greatness in your counterpart and believe they are capable of greatness and make efforts towards that goal. There are some FSF counterparts who truly lack either the capacity, vision, or the motivation to be great at their job. However, most FSF want to be stellar performers and help them. By accepting a product that meets baseline standards, is not good enough for a professional soldier. A truly professional soldier is dedicated to improving the security of his people and protecting his own national security interests.

As a corollary, some advisors fall into the folly of forcing an American standard onto an indigenous system. Initially, this may even appear to be successful. However, ultimately the result will include unsustainable solutions. For example, what separates the US Army from other armies is our capacity for detailed staff analysis and planning. We are not as command-centric as our FSF counterparts in Iraq and Afghanistan where the entire unit adopts the attitudes of the FSF Commander.

For example, inexperienced US units have attempted to force the Military Decision Making Process (MDMP) onto the FSF unit they are working with. This was a horrendous mistake.

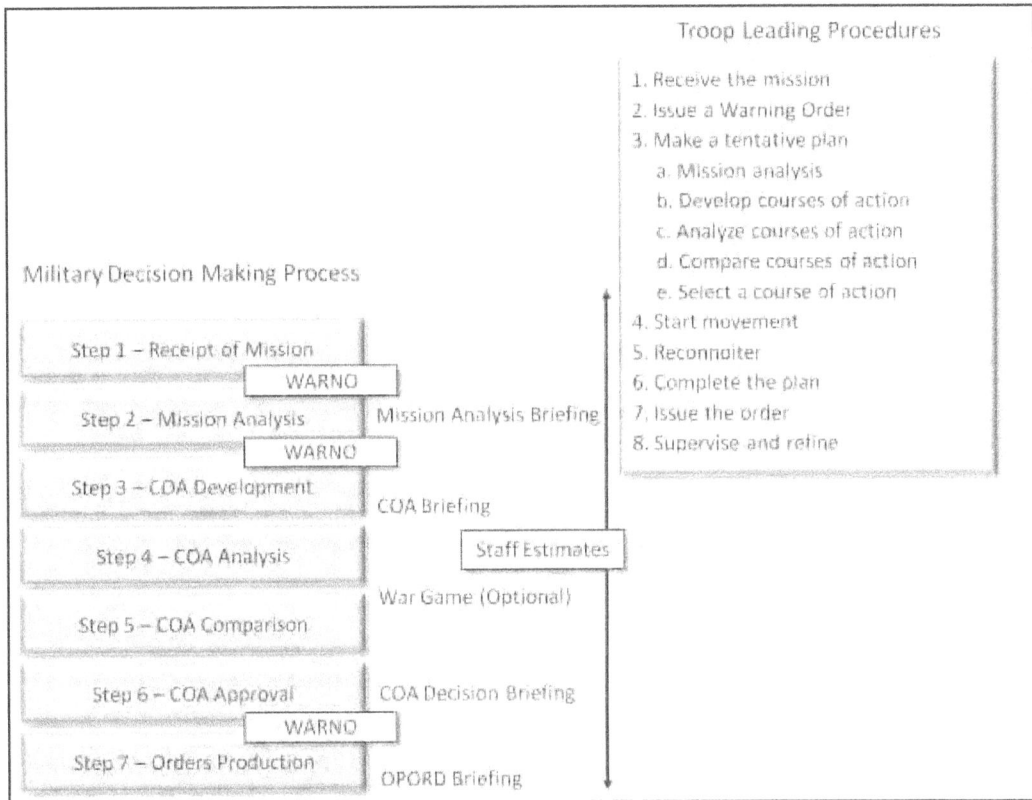

Figure 35. MDMP based on US doctrine, forms the basis of our tactical operations planning process. It requires good staff analysis and estimates provided to the commander for decisions.

The MDMP is effective when a well trained staff has access to accurate, detailed, and timely information regarding their own capabilities, the enemy status, and the civilian population stance. This is not the case in most other militaries and particularly in the Iraqi and Afghan units I have worked with. By and large, with the command-centric decision-making authority models used in many other militaries, staff officers fail to receive very accurate information. They do not permit the concept of fulfilling the commander's intent as justification for unilateral missions. Organizations are often compartmentalized or insulated.

The FSF normally have a planning process. As an advisor, we must learn their system and see where we can improve it as long as the FSF unit requests such training. For example, the Iraqi Military Staff College, which is 12 months long, trains the UK "Combat

Estimate" system as a result of being dominated by the UK military when they were formed into a country in 1922. This Combat Estimate system works well in the Iraqi military as well as other militaries, as it reinforces the commander's decision-making primacy and is ultimately faster to plan an operation than using the MDMP (though arguably it contains less detailed staff estimates).

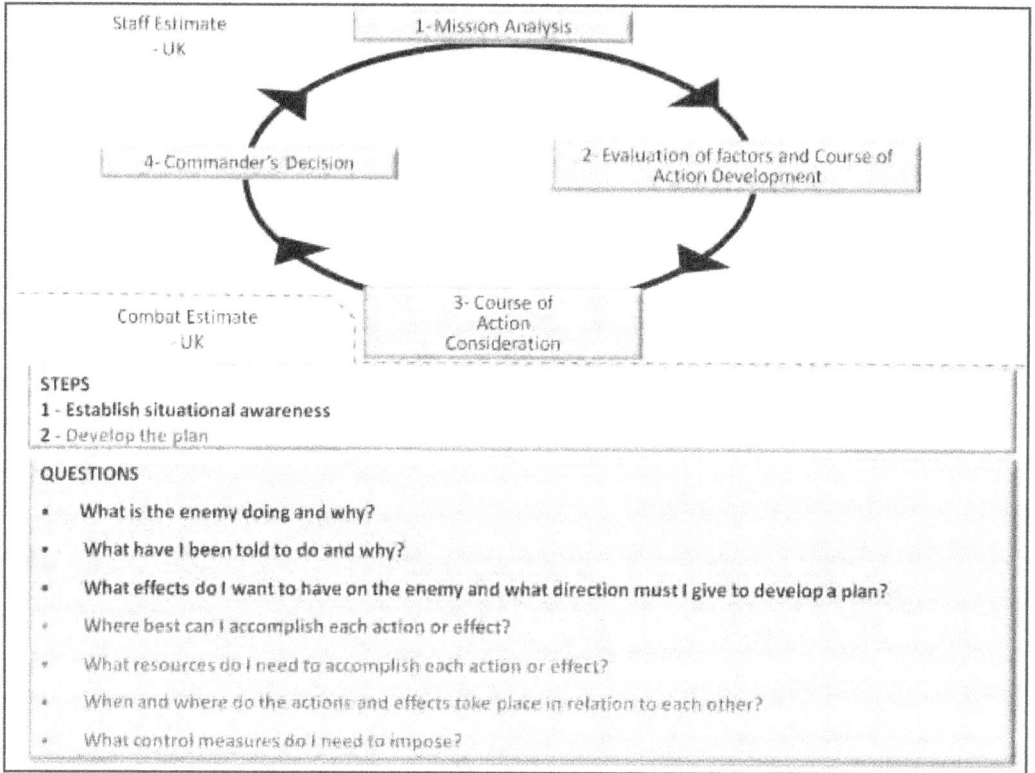

Figure 36. Combat Estimate (UK model) is the process taught in the Iraqi Military Staff College. It heavily relies upon the commander's understanding of the situation and answering seven questions.

Another peril advisors face is taking personal responsibility for the FSF performance. Remember, advisors do not command. The FSF is accountable for its own actions. This is a tough delineation for some US partners to accept if the US advisors are with the FSF 24/7. The US partner units should remember the FSF does not report to them or the US advisors. The US advisors will never be privy to every action the FSF conducts nor will they be able to accurately observe each engagement with the enemy or the people. Some US advisors burn themselves out by their inability to focus on the areas which can most benefit their FSF counterparts. As an American advisor, your duty is to coach, teach, mentor, liaise, observe, assist, prepare, train, or facilitate and not to command or direct the FSF.

Be cautious when dealing with a reluctant counterpart. Not all FSF counterparts are as open and amiable to American advisors as our general. In fact, he was the best I have worked with. One of my best friends recently advised another FSF counterpart, who was most often indifferent to the advice or presence of the American advisor team. Some days the FSF counterpart appeared hostile but mostly he was evasive. This presents a new challenge for us. How do you successfully fulfill your military duties by offering advice and assistance to a FSF counterpart who does not want it?

The answer is to make your advice beneficial to the FSF counterpart. First, establish what the FSF counterpart values. What pictures are in his office? What books are on the table? What does he talk about? What badges are on his uniform? What does he show interest in personally and professionally? These may not always be apparent things but the answers are sitting in the room with you. Advising is as much a personal investment and friendship as it is a professional venture. Next, determine what resources and assets you and your team can provide to your counterpart. In addition to the list of enablers, your team has some special skills which are not always readily apparent.

For example, one advisor team noticed the FSF was unfamiliar with the maintenance for a new western style vehicle their unit received. The FSF mechanics were illiterate and could not read the maintenance manuals nor were spare parts readily available. As a result, the new trucks would either sit in the motor pools under lock and key, or the FSF would be drive them until they broke and then abandoned them on the side of the road. Fortunately, one of the US advisors, though not a mechanic, had a brother in the car business. Through the advisor's brother, the team wrote to the vehicle manufacturer and obtained a picture book of the maintenance procedures from schematic design drawings. FSF used the picture book as a coloring book which helped the FSF mechanics learn the systems of the new truck in a similar way that medical students apply the book of Gray's Anatomy. Also, the advisor worked diligently through the logistics system in order to establish a small stock of common repair parts. As a result of these efforts and with support of the chain of command, the trucks were slowly returned to an operational readiness rate of 70 percent by the end of the tour which was up from 25 percent.

Next, do not get "snowed" by reports from your FSF counterpart. Many military cultures have a "zero defects" mentality where it is inconceivable and inexcusable to report accurate shortages, let alone fail a mission. For example, if our current FSF counterparts report one of their vehicles as 'damaged' they will lose the fuel rations for that vehicle from their chain of command. Accordingly, counterparts do not report vehicles as damaged, despite serious mechanical deficiencies. Therefore, many reports are never logged properly or are devilishly inaccurate. As an advisor, seeing is believing and be careful you do not accept everything on paper as opposed to hard reality and baseline evidence. We must validate reports as delicately and efficiently as possible without jeopardizing our relationship.

A variation of getting "snowed" is dealing with a corrupt unit. For example, the legitimate government does not control some FSF military units at all rather they are overrun with militia influence or loyalty to a particular warlord. This happens on today's battlefields, so how should we respond?

As an example, I led a US advisor team in 2006 during the 'bad days' in Iraq where our FSF counterparts were heavily influenced by the *Shi'a* militia known as *Jayish Al-Mahdi* or JAM (Army of the Messiah). As evidence mounted, it implicated the FSF unit was undeniably corrupt and our US advisor team was placed in the dangerous position. Our FSF counterparts were not interested in the security for all local citizens. They were working toward population redistribution by targeting Sunni civilians and forcing them from their homes while consolidating power for JAM by terrorizing local citizens. Still, we had a duty to maintain situational awareness of the unit for the US Forces and to make every attempt to mitigate the impact of militia infiltration which was counterproductive to providing security in the area. Each time we advisors gathered evidence which exposed such corruption within the unit; another ISF commander would take charge which was more ineffective than the previous one. This continued through six battalion commanders until the entire brigade was disbanded and retrained … twice at a training facility in Numaniyah, Iraq. The overall unit status and the entire attitude of the unit improved dramatically by the end of the surge period in late 2007 when the brigade leadership and key leaders ultimately changed.

This begs the question, "Are there acceptable levels of corruption which we can deal with for our western mindset?" I believe this is a question of perception. What we as Americans perceive as corruption, some FSF interpret it as the cost of doing business! For example, is it corrupt to falsely report a vehicle status as "operational" when the transmission is blown and the vehicle is used for spare parts? Failure to accurately report such a deadline deficiency is punishable in the US and why shouldn't we scream "FOUL!" in Iraq? As we stated earlier, the fuel rations will be cut from any unit reporting such a vehicle deficiency, understanding the operational rate numbers will be hyper-inflated for the units.

What about if the advisor team witnesses FSF unit extorting money from the local citizens at a checkpoint? This is a direct violation of the FSF duties to protect the people. However, several examples of "toll roads" exist in Afghanistan. Along country roads, there is an expected tribute which people expect to pay to the Afghanistan National Security Force (ANSF) or *Arbakai* guarding the roads. Is this acceptable?

The rules must be clear from the chain of command as to how to react and report to such challenges. In my personal opinion, it is noteworthy to mention the first example regarding the false operational readiness reporting (we do) but we do not take any administrative action beyond understanding the problems for situational awareness. In the second example, the practice of "toll roads" is unacceptable to me as it directly affects the people the FSF are attempting to secure. The FSF receive their pay through their chain of command and rely upon maintaining a good relationship with the local people if they are to be effective and supported.

The extreme side of getting "snowed" is of course, "going native." This is never acceptable. Living within the culture is good, whereas forsaking your country is not. For example, if a higher US command directs an operation, the advisor is duty bound to work to accomplish it within the parameters of his role as an advisor. Advisors do not command the Foreign Security Forces. The principal example of this stemmed from some criticisms of T.E. Lawrence going native. Given the particular circumstances of Lawrence's nebulous tasks and guidance from a British command authority which was hundreds of miles away, he was forced to adopt many of the customs and the attire of his Arab guerilla forces in order accomplish the mission. Our present military force structure and support mechanisms for advisor teams should prevent this from occurring in the modern battlefield.

Accordingly, when told to paint our HWWMVs similar to the marking of our IA counterparts in order to maintain a low US signature, we asked for a verbal or written directive from our chain of command. We were not going to be accused of going off the reservation. We asked for explicit guidance and directives in order to ensure we stayed within the boundaries of our commander's intent.

We are not trying to create an Iraqi Army in our image nor should we expect to become an Iraqi Army. The IA has a proud tradition and history as does our American forces and do not betray either of them by adopting your counterparts viewpoint as the only truth. Your counterpart relies upon your American professionalism and perspective. Do not violate that duty in the hopes of gaining greater acceptance into the FSF mindset. Once assimilated into the FSF, you are no longer an asset to your counterpart. There is a line between sincere respect and blind subservience and do not cross it. Do not violate your national integrity or the faith the American people have placed in you. Your value as an American advisor is more prized than any desires of complete acceptance into the FSF culture.

Section VII

Is SFA a Universal Solution?

Though a global effort exists to stamp out terrorist havens, the current struggles in Iraq and Afghanistan are radically different. The terrain, the people, the enemy, the indigenous government architecture, and the root causes of insurgency differ in almost every respect. How can we hope to successfully apply the same solution to the uncommon challenges?

With the advent of emerging SFA doctrine (FM 3-07.1), the shifting US military has experimented with different organizational roles in Foreign Internal Defense (FID). We have used Special Operations Forces (SOF), US Marine platoon, ad hoc US Army Military Transition Teams, civilian police and customs agents, US Border Patrol agents, civilian contractors, etc. In this era of persistent conflict, should our profession consider SFA, particularly military advising, as a universal solution to doing more with less? In this, some have suggested that the only path to victory is by encouraging the indigenous forces to secure their own population and through limited advisor and partnership assistance, to establish professional standards for the military, reinforce the FSF strengths, help the FSF through their shortcomings, and provide them with the necessary legitimacy to secure the people.

Designing new maneuver units and organizations specifically to conduct security force assistance or SFA has been suggested by military strategists, civilian think tanks, the US Congress, and others. The US Military Institutions however, are reticent to adopting the "Advise and Assist" mantra as a systemic vehicle for waging fourth generation warfare. The institution prefers to test the flexibility of the modular Brigade Combat Team augmented for SFA missions rather than institutionalize an organic Corps of Advisors to enhance their warfighting and peace enforcement capabilities. To this I say, "Three bags full." so long as we train for SFA missions when appropriate and our Combined Training Centers (CTC) rotations have the flexibility to adapt to test those skill sets. We have witnessed great improvements in this area. However, the mindset is still tough to adjust when placed in an assistance role as opposed to straight conventional warfighting.

SFA operations are the preferred method of engagement in the counterinsurgencies of today in Afghanistan and Iraq. However, they are conducted using different architectures, different levels of partnership, and different levels of understanding by our forces as well as those we are working with to be honest. Prior to launching a SFA mission as opposed to a different method of engagement, leaders and planners must understand the personalities of the FSF, the capabilities of the FSF, and the environment (in terms of people and physical terrain).

The best conditions for a SFA mission is if:

The key FSF personalities accept incremental responsibility for the security in the area and are willing to work with the advisors and partner units to enhance their professionalism.

The FSF are capable of operating by providing local area security in limited capacity of company-level and below for an extended period.

The people will support a professional indigenous security force (military, para-military, or police) with some western influence to be responsible for their security and the physical terrain is conducive to protecting the people from external actors subversion and interference.

In the 1980s, American involvement in El Salvador was a hallmark case study for successful SFA. With a Congressionally mandated cap of 355 advisors which could be engaged on the ground in El Salvador on a daily basis, the El Salvadoran military successfully routed the attacks of a communist dominated insurgency. The counterinsurgency operations and rules governing these American advisors shifted over time. However, we achieved our ultimate goal as the US Special Forces and intelligence agency teams assisted the El Salvadoran forces to drive the communist insurgents from the cities and pursue them in the jungles of Central America.

SFA is not the panacea for fourth generation warfare. Rather, SFA is a proven method for maintaining our national security interests with a small low profile footprint. As we have discussed, these three conditions for supporting a SFA program exist in Iraq today and other theaters of operations are different and have their unique challenges.

"We [USF and ISF] are further down the road with SFA here [in Iraq] than in Afghanistan. We are now setting the stage for strategic relationships."
Colonel Roger Cloutier, Commander, 1/3 AAB

In this era of persistent conflict, pundits and military analysts have suggested that through a robust training program, we can functionally make US combat troops unnecessary in our current warzones. However, when you put that plan from paper into action, there are some significant challenges that leaders and planners take into account.

Based on this rudimentary comparison of the challenges both countries face in their counterinsurgency efforts, it is unclear if conditions exist where Security Force Assistance missions should overshadow traditional counterinsurgency operations in Afghanistan.

Fortunately, General David Petraeus, the man who engineered great success in Iraq's counterinsurgency efforts, accepted a position to assume command in Afghanistan at a critical time. In 2010, General Petraeus issued his Counterinsurgency Guidance for Afghanistan, which built upon the principles tested and validated in Iraq when he served and the Commanding General of Multi-National Forces and Iraq (MNF-I) in July 2008. Further, in August 2010, General Petraeus issued counter-insurgency or COIN Qualification Standards for Afghanistan which clearly depicted how to train the deploying forces into Afghanistan, highlighting the unique nature of Afghanistan and the NATO coalition warfare.

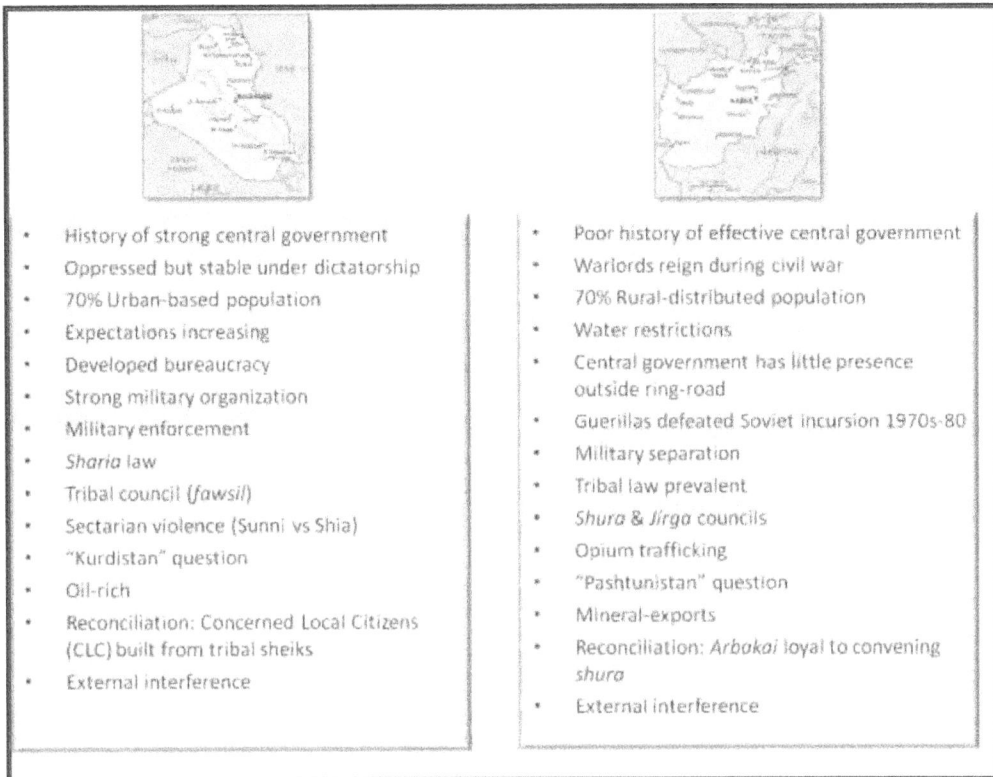

Figure 37. Comparison between Iraq and Afghanistan.

• History of strong central government	• Poor history of effective central government
• Oppressed but stable under dictatorship	• Warlords reign during civil war
• 70% Urban-based population	• 70% Rural-distributed population
• Expectations increasing	• Water restrictions
• Developed bureaucracy	• Central government has little presence outside ring-road
• Strong military organization	• Guerillas defeated Soviet incursion 1970s-80
• Military enforcement	• Military separation
• *Sharia* law	• Tribal law prevalent
• Tribal council (*fawsil*)	• *Shura* & *Jirga* councils
• Sectarian violence (Sunni vs Shia)	• Opium trafficking
• "Kurdistan" question	• "Pashtunistan" question
• Oil-rich	• Mineral-exports
• Reconciliation: Concerned Local Citizens (CLC) built from tribal sheiks	• Reconciliation: *Arbakai* loyal to convening *shura*
• External interference	• External interference

In Afghanistan, there is a poor track record of a central governing body extending past the main cities and ring road which connects them. In 2008, seven years after the US led coalition began combat operations against Al Qaeda, a combined American and Afghanistan National Army (US-ANA) patrol reached a remote mountain village and was met by several gun toting villagers who were surprised at the presence of the Americans and they expressed pleasure that we had helped run out the Soviets in the area. However, the village pleasantly welcomed the combined patrol and professed only a rumored knowledge of Taliban control or any understanding of recent changes in the government. They were content to tend their subsistence farms and very limited market activity. After departing, the ANA patrol leader commented, "We will probably never go back there and those people do not need us. We will leave them alone."

It's tough to champion the primacy of indigenous security forces when the premise of central government authority is not accepted. The FSF are after all, the enforcing element of the legitimate central authority. This is tough to adapt to in the tribally dominated areas outside the major cities.

75

Figure 38. Afghan National Security Forces on patrol in Nuristan in 2008.

US advisor teams have made an enormous impact under the guidance of the Combined Security and Training Command and Afghanistan (CSTC-A). The advisors or Embedded Training Teams (ETTs) at the tactical command-level, work with all elements of the Afghan National Security Forces (ANSF). These ETTs are different from the MiTTs in Iraq however, and they are larger in size and their command relationships are separate from the US partnering units. This is difficult to change as some of the ETTs are composed of troops from another NATO allied country as Operation Enduring Freedom (OEF) evolved into a NATO command in 2004. This adds layers of bureaucracy to the already difficult chain of command and the ETTs and NATO Observer Mentor Liaison Teams (OMLTs) operate in the spider web threads of authority, command, and responsibility surrounding the Regional Commands.

When compared to the current situation in Iraq, Afghanistan requires different rules for the advisor-partner-FSF counterpart relationship. The ETTs perform more direct training of the Afghan National Army, Afghan National Police (ANP) and Afghan Border Police (ABP). In general and for a variety of reasons, I believe the ANSF need this more direct supervision and heavy advisor presence in order to ensure they maintain standards and to train a culture of professionalism, which is sustainable from the central government authority in Afghanistan.

Figure 39. US advisors training Afghan Security Forces in Logar Province in 2007.

Regardless of who is in power, this is an opportunity for the local tribal authorities to participate in an organized central government which can effectively run the country and be an international partner to neighboring nations as well as being a regional power. This ties in to meeting the expectations of the people and providing access to essential services while maintaining order for the Afghans. SFA is a way to this end, if the SFA/FID imperatives are applied (see Appendix C: SFA/FID Imperatives). Today, Special Operations Command (USSOCOM), as the proponent for SFA within the Department of Defense, is generating US Forces Security Force Assistance Training and Qualification Standards which promise to be a beacon for our sustained understanding of how we must prepare our future advisor forces.

The general was discussing the future of American forces in Iraq during an office call with a prominent US general in Baghdad. The US general asked, "*Sadee*, what do you think will happen when the US forces leave Iraq after 2011?"

"We still want the US forces here," the general stated openly as he tapped out another cigarette into the golden ashtray. "We have made such combined sacrifices together, the US troops, Iraqi soldiers, police, and most importantly the Iraqi civilians. We have some peace now but we have paid for this peace with our combined blood. It is time to put the Americans in the back of the fight and let the Iraqis stand in front. It is our country and our honor but we still need you here."

Figure 40. US advisors and ANSF on patrol in Logar Province in 2007.

The US general responded, "We have fought alongside each other for several years and sacrificed much. We are your partners but it is our understanding, based on the current Security Agreement, that the US forces will go back the America after December 2011. Your forces are strong."

The general continued, "I believe our new government will ask the Americans to stay. The impression the Americans have made on the Iraqi people is huge. Most do not want you to leave either. Ask them, 'What do the Americans do?' and they say, 'The Americans build, they crushed the dictator Saddam. Now, they give us money, jobs, training, schools, and a better life. How could we hate them?'"

"Now, I am not a politician," the general said "but if I was in charge, I would ask to keep an American division or two [about 30,000 troops] on five bases across the country. These would not be combat forces though. They would be advisors and witnesses. They would watch over and support our Iraqi forces as we grow. They would protect our Iraqi democracy and our people. We still have enemies outside our borders which will come after us if you leave. They have seen that democracy can work here and they are threatened so they will start trouble in Iraq. Of course, coups and violent revolution has been part of our history for the last 1,400 years. It will take a generation to settle that passion and we cannot change that mentality in eight years. We still need you [Americans]. "When you have a beautiful garden, we do not want to open it to just anyone who is around. They will each cut flowers for themselves. We need the Americans to help us tend the garden, and we will cut the weeds."

Figure 41. ANSF and civilian officials in Panshir, Afghanistan in 2008.

The US general conceded, "No doubt we will remain a partner and a friend. The scope of that friendship has yet to be determined. The crucial part of this is the violent militias [violent extremist networks] who target the Iraqi people and our combined security forces. They must be reduced."

The general lit another cigarette and concluded, "The future is always better and this is true. The American forces should transfer the combat forces into advisor forces and witnesses and you will witness history. Your forces should observe and record what happens here. You have eyes and ears and a mind to think and you are the witnesses."

Responses from an Iraqi Commanding General

Sadee, there are a few questions we are struggling with. We would appreciate any insights you could offer to us.

The following are the notes from several conversations with our Iraqi counterpart, who is in charge of an Iraqi Army Division of more than 10,000 Soldiers in the southern Baghdad belt sector of Mahmudiyah which is a rural sprawling area the size of Jacksonville, Florida containing about 500,000 people.

What is the condition of the Iraqi Army? Is it able to defend its citizens from an external invasion?

We can stand on our own for our internal security but that is not what we need from the Army. The Army should be focused on the enemies of our country and outside our country. We still need American help to get there. Not a large force but we need a group of Americans who remain here to help us train and sustain ourselves. We are not yet able to transfer internal security to the Police forces.

How does the Iraqi Security Force secure their population? How do the Iraqis disrupt and attack the terrorist networks and drivers of instability? What are the critical pieces you need to attack a network?

We need intelligence, real-time and accurate. If you can tell me where a target is, and why he is bad, I can get him off the street and into a judge's warrant.

How do the Iraqi police and Iraqi Army work together?

Today, I have a memorandum signed by the Prime Minister that states that the Police forces in southern Baghdad belt report to the Iraqi Army (IA). It will not always be this way but today, they are too weak to stand alone. The IA has to be the force today but we need the Police and the *sawah* as they represent the faces of the people in the area.

How do the people behave when they feel secure?

The people here feel secure. I know because they let their children play in the streets. There is no fear in them and they respect the ISF (Iraqi Security Forces).

Why are there so many checkpoints (over 300 in this rural area), instead of more dynamic foot patrols in the area?

We agree the TCPs (traffic control points) are defensive positions. We were not going to reduce the number of TCPs before the national elections of March 7, 2010, however because if a VBIED (Vehicle Born Improvised Explosive Device) exploded after reducing our security posture, then we would be blamed. We have worked too hard and sacrificed too much to be blamed for such an attack. After elections were over, we reduced 10% of our TCPs. After all, the TCPs really hurt the civilians who are traveling on the roads and not the terrorists who normally use side roads or travel during peak times on main roads when there is little chance of being searched. After elections, we will reduce TCPs about 10% each month until we have only 150 TCPs in the area. With the extra manpower, we built patrol bases and a platoon-sized quick response force for each Battalion. The *jundi* (low-level soldier/independent patrol) need to get off the TCPs too. Some joined the Iraqi Army over five years ago and have been sitting on TCPs ever since. They need to get back to soldier tasks and ambushes, raids, and patrols.

How do you measure your effectiveness for offensive and defensive operations?

We know we are successful when the women and children are in the streets without supervision. We know we are successful when you plug in a radio and it works. We know we are successful when the farms are green and the food prices are low.

What are your priorities, as a Commander?

We need several things in order to be successful. Some are clearly more important than others. Mostly, we need improved access to more accurate Intelligence such as databases, video surveillance, human networks. With better intelligence and source networks, we can project limited forces and intercept the criminals and terrorists before they act. We also need more reliable communications with radios and antennas, better vehicles and equipment for Soldiers (HWMMVs, tankers, 5-ton trucks, construction and engineering equipment, EOD (ordnance disposal) specialty equipment, weapons, global positioning GPS, night vision devices, improved training standards and advanced techniques to include general Soldier standards for training as well as specialty certification courses for medics and EOD and staff section procedures, base upgrades and quality of life for Soldiers and Officers with base improvements and road construction.

Where does the Iraqi Army require the most assistance from the American Forces?

The Iraqi Army needs to learn self reliance and self sustainment from the Americans. This is the most important lesson for the ISF. Some Iraqi Officers see the Army as a paycheck and they do not care if they do not train or have good weapons. We need to first love our job to serve and a few of us sincerely do. This cannot be taught, however. The reason why the Americans have the best Army in the world is they love their job. They are completely loyal to their country and their people love them. This is where we want to be. In the old regime, we had about 54 Divisions and we do not want that Army again. Today we have about 14 Divisions and that is enough with the right amount of tanks, artillery, and aircraft. Right now we do not have the equipment to stand alone to defend our own people. We must build to serve this new Army and we need a generation to grow and change our mentality. We still need you [Americans].

How do you use the American advisors? What do you want or need from them?

I need two things from the American advisors. I need a military professional and a witness to what we are doing here. I mean, I want the advisor's counsel and honest opinion about how to get things accomplished in the Division. I need the advisor's help pushing for camp improvements, maintaining equipment, and training the staff and specialty teams of course but I also need the US advisor to witness how we are working and I want the advisor with us every day. That way, when false accusations are leveled against us, the advisor can say, "I was with the general when that incident allegedly occurred and it is a lie." You are Americans with no reason to lie and you tell the truth. Sometimes you don't know any better.

How do you get it?

Every day, you are welcome here. I talk to "Jim" everyday too and even on Fridays if I am not around the camp or on *jaza* (leave). The advisor has to go with me to every official engagement. We travel together and I prefer to have the advisors in my vehicle. That way we can talk on the way to a meeting. The American PSD (personal security detachment/detail) can follow us, if the advisor thinks it's necessary.

Today, where is the best place for the American Advisors to assist the IA Division? As the numbers of American Force reduce, should the advisors focus on the Operations Centers or logistical systems or working directly with the senior Iraqi Commanders?

We need access to better intelligence and training on intelligence systems or network analysis. This is the most important thing we get from the American forces. Today, the advisor team gives me the INTEL reports each day in English and Iraqi Arabic. This helps both of us build the picture for the G2 intelligence and the plan operations. If there is something like a weapons cache report that is accurate enough, we will act on it immediately. If the information is outside of my division's sector, I will call the division commander who controls the area and pass the INTEL to him directly. The Operations Center is where we keep a small American presence to pass routine information. This is how we battle-track our daily operations. Bigger operations require more planning and thought so some plans are developed over a few days in my office. I will tell the staff what to do and their job is to do it.

What are unforgivable mistakes you have seen from the American Forces?

Some of the Americans working with Iraqi Army have made terrible mistakes. What angers us most is when they treat us without respect. That is unforgivable. Without respect, there is no trust.

Do the Americans demonstrate the ability and willingness to learn about you and your Iraqi Army unit?

This [American] Division, this Brigade, this Task Force and this Advisor team understand who we are. They are genuine and sincere and they want to help our Iraqi Division fight and protect the people. Past American units have tried to do this by themselves without our help and this was a mistake. Only an Iraqi force should secure Iraqi people.

How do you balance personal curiosity with professional understanding?

We want the Americans to understand us. We are one unit and one family here. There is no gap between us. Of course you will make mistakes and so will we but always work with respect in mind. If you show us the respect we deserve, we will work with you. The American units who fail to show us respect for our sacrifices are isolated. We may be ordered to work in the same area but we will not really work together with them.

What should the American forces learn before they arrive in your country to work with you and your organization?

As American forces train to come into this country to work with us, they must have some basic knowledge and understanding of the Iraqi Army and culture. Most importantly, they need to realize that we have worked with Americans before but this is our country. Our laws and systems are in effect and not yours.

In December 2011, what should the relationship be with the American Forces? The American government and its armed forces want to establish a sincere long-term relationship with the Iraqi Army. How can we achieve this?

I would ask to keep an American Division or two of about 30,000 troops on five bases across the country. These are not combat forces though. They would be advisors and witnesses. They would watch over and support our Iraqi forces as we grow. They would protect our Iraqi democracy and our people. We still have enemies outside our borders which will come after us if you leave. They have seen that democracy can work here and they are threatened so they will start trouble in Iraq. Of course, coups and violent revolution has been part of our history for the last 1,400 years. It will take a generation to settle that passion and we cannot change that mentality in eight years. We still need you [Americans].

Section IX

Summary

Today's American Army was born from the training and advice of our European allies combined with our American brand of fierce self determination. This warrior ethos has morphed into our approach to military advising, particularly in today's combat zones.

We have proposed several maxims as to how to shape your relationship with your FSF counterparts. Successful advising begins with studying doctrine and case studies from past advisors. Ask yourself, "How would I do this better in X country?" Then apply those lessons in reality-based training vignettes. These are readily accomplished through the folks of the 162d ITB, the JFK Special Warfare Center, the US Marine Corps Advisor Training Group at 29 Palms, the US Air Force Air Advisor Academy, the Joint Center for International Security Force Assistance (JCISFA), NATO's Joint Forces Training Center (JFTC) in Poland, and other quality training sites. Contact these experts, even if you cannot attend a full course with your unit. Advising is a perishable skill and cross-cultural training from different outlets is always a great way to learn. Demonstrate your organizational adaptability and look further than the "task, conditions, and standards" model of US Army training mantra. Get creative.

Generate a durable relationship. This is the essence of advising. Remember, you are a guest in their country. It is their responsibility to protect their indigenous population. As advisors, we provide leadership, access to enablers, and direct combat assistance in order to promote FSF professionalism and legitimacy. The role of the combat advisor is constrained by your direct lines of operation and your imagination of how to fulfill the objectives together. Relationships here are a "pacing" item and require careful attention. Further, advisors should advise, train, assist, and equip their counterparts as appropriate in order to establish, improve, or reinforce the existing indigenous systems and procedures. We are not building an American military.

Improve your team each day. Advisors must talk to each other across a "flattened" organization in order to share success and acknowledge challenges. Advisors cross train each other in order to reinforce the professional development of their team. On the negative side, advisor teams are notoriously small, which means you cannot hide cowardice, incompetence, or apathy. If any member of the advisor team suffers from such a character flaw, marginalize him immediately. A wise man once said, "You can lead a horse to water but you cannot make him drink." If a member of your advisor team refuses to drink the water despite training, guidance, and directives to play nicely, then keep him away from other good members of your team. People who refuse to listen, learn, and apply are terrible advisors and their expertise lies elsewhere.

Look for opportunities to improve your counterpart's existing capabilities. Know what your capabilities and limitations are and know your counterpart's command priorities. Understand that a modest improvement of a capability – such as building a more capable strike force, bomb disposal company, maintenance ordering procedures, route clearance team, or intelligence analysis – can inspire other units to follow and emulate that success. This can lead to a significant improvement to the counterpart's institutional system.

Be wary of the perils and pitfalls of becoming too rigid or too comfortable in your position as an advisor. This is far and away the best job you could ever hope for if you stay within the lines of your commander's guidance. Your goals should complement the US partner and FSF unit commander's priorities. The combined understanding of how to provide access, support, and enablers is your battle drill. You must react quickly and decisively when asked for assistance without jumping into a pool with the lights off and the water may have been drained the evening prior.

Advising is not the only tool in the warfighting arsenal. However, it is an area where we have rediscovered an aptitude for success. I pray these lessons stay with us through the future wars.

Appendix A

S-TT Tactical Standing Operating Procedures (TACSOP)

This TACSOP was developed for the first fully resourced AAB in Baghdad which covered seven Iraqi Security Force (ISF) Divisions and three area commands from January 2010 to January 2011. It incorporates a 127 slide presentation which we used to accompany pre-mission training and refined after 60 days in theater.

Topic   Sub-Topic

Maps

      Area of Interest

      Area of Responsibility

TOC Operations

      Integration of Tasks

      Duty Descriptions

      Adjacent Unit Coordination

      Patrol Brief

      Patrol Debrief

      Battle Rhythm

      Target Synchronization Matrix

      CoIST Intelligence Timeline / TOC Set-Up Requirements

      Roll Call for Meetings

   Tactical Operations

      Troop Leading Procedures / Military Decision Making Process

      Staff Estimate – UK / Combat Estimate – UK

      Post Mission Procedures

      9 Principles of ED Combat

      Truck Configuration

      Movement Formations

      Crew Drills

        React to Ambush

        Block Ambush

        React to IED / VBIED

        CASEVAC

Replacement Gunner

Replace Driver

Disabled Vehicle

Tire Change

Long Halt

3 Point Turn / Reverse Out

Rollover

Dismount / Mount

React to Sniper

Vehicle Pull Over / Snap TCP

TCP Vehicle Search

Overpass

Intersection

Entry Control Point

Danger Area

Movement through Building

Center-Fed Room

Corner-Fed Room

Room Clearing

Close-Quarters Marksmanship

Detainee Operations

Cordon & Search

Force Protection

Risk Management / Risk Reduction

Weapons Control Status

Load Plan

Culture and Considerations

RFIs

First Meeting Guidance

Iraqi Phrases / Alphabet

Islamic Calendar

Iraqi Counterpart Family Summary

Key Leader Engagement Preparation Sheet

Combat Capabilities Tracker

Command and Control

> SOI
>
> Communications – Command Post / Tactical
>
> Succession of Command
>
> Communications Standards

Reports

> S-TT Report Requirements
>
> LACE/SALT
>
> IED/UXO
>
> Iraqi Air/Ground MEDEVAC and Casualty Checklist
>
> 9-Line MEDEVAC Request
>
> US Field Medical Card
>
> Call for Fire / CAS Briefing Form
>
> Close Air Support Basic 9-Line
>
> Close Combat Attack
>
> CCF / CCA Blank Request

References and Tools

> S-TT CONOP Checklist
>
> S-TT Information Requirements
>
> Checklists
>
> Command Relationship / C2 Structure
>
> S-TT Task Organization
>
> S-TT Coverage Plan
>
> Significant Event Tracker
>
> Equipment and Personnel Tracking Sheets
>
> Upcoming Meeting Tracker
>
> Classes of Supply Tracker
>
> S-TT BUB Update Slide
>
> Working Group Input
>
> Computer Reporting Possibilities
>
> Media Talking Points
>
> 5988-E Example

SWEAT Analysis

ROE Card

JAG Guidance Card

Air Support Procedures

Crater Analysis Class

Site Exploitation Smart Card

Company Input to Battalion Targeting

Security Force Assistance Construct

Websites and References

Appendix B

Planning Standing Operational Procedure (SOP) for Foreign Security Force (FSF)

Planning Cell

The purpose of this planning SOP is to describe the actions of the special staff element in the planning process during Security Force Assistance (SFA) missions.

In the advent of SFA, the Battalion and Higher echelon staffs do not have an organic structure to fully employ the FSF circumstances and situation. This is increasingly important as we are assuming that modular Brigade Combat Teams (BCTs) are able to accept augmentation for SFA missions without training or much guidance. Emerging doctrine has helped the effort, such as FM 3-07.1, Security Force Assistance (May 2009), and the US Infantry School's Handbook for Commanders on Security Force Assistance (June 2009). This planning SOP provides some specific planning considerations and tasks for FSF Planning Cell and guidance for the Stability-Transition Teams (S-TTs), who will execute the plan.

Characteristics of the FSF Planners: should have prior experience working with Foreign Security Forces (FSF) such as Transition Team, Embedded Training Team, Liaison Officer, Foreign Area Specialist, etc. Further, the FSF Planners should have a desire to improve the FSF systems dynamically as the S-TTs can operate autonomously (not independently) and report collectively to the organizational headquarters.

For 1-3 HBCT, the proponent of the FSF Planning Cell is the S3 (Operations Officer) with critical input from the Provost Marshal Officer (PMO).

Mission Analysis (MA). During this planning phase, the FSF Planners will:

- Pursue Requests for Further Information (RFIs).

- Provide FSF lay down (location, composition, and disposition) of all assets and resources (capabilities) identified for FSF support in the operational environment.

- Provide FSF unit locations, FSF key personalities (biographies), general history of FSF units, current operational responsibilities, FSF battlespace, and unit assessments (Operational Readiness Assessments or ORA).

- Provide list of US available: Partnership units, S-TT, Law Enforcement Professionals (LEPs), Human Terrain Teams (HTTs), Intelligence Surveillance Reconnaissance (ISR) platforms, etc.

- Detail US roles and responsibilities of partnership units, advisor team, and augmenting elements. Identify the critical command relationships early.

- Capture initial elements into WARNO#2.

- *During MA Brief: Conduct Intelligence Preparation of the Battlefield (IPB) of FSF laydown, FSF personalitie,s and US assets available. Frame the "M" – "Military" in the PMESII-PT.*

Course of Action (COA) Development. During this planning phase, the FSF Planners will:

- Pursue Requests for Further Information (RFIs). Think ahead of the subordinate elements, "What do they need to know and understand in order to be effective?"

- Describe FSF steady-state operations and project FSF missions based upon upcoming events and concept of assistance.

- Identify Drivers of Instability as they relate to the FSF. Align the FSF in the Lines of Effort (weighting the Main Effort).

- Propose task and purpose of US partnership units and advisor teams (S-TTs). Identify Measures of Performance (MoP) and Measures of Effectiveness (MoE) for each task and purpose. Match these to the Lines of Effort, in order to generate specified and assigned tasks.

- Input information into risk management (operational and tactical levels). Identify standards of discipline and conduct. Balance force protection with risk shared with the FSF (e.g., weapon status, uniform, Combined TACSOP with FSF).

- Identify key pieces of FSF equipment (e.g. artillery, mortars, small arms, radios, personal protective equipment, etc). Understand these systems and tools and be able to use them alongside the FSF.

- Identify critical training requirements if applicable (e.g., Money as a Weapon System, Combat Lifesaver, Negotiation, & Influence, etc.)

- *During COA Development Brief: Refined FSF lay down and proposed partner unit/advisor team coverage (including task, purpose, MoP and MoE). Identify Drivers of Instability within the lines of effort, concept of support (to include C2 relationships, vertical and lateral coordination requirements).*

Wargaming Phase.

- Adopt the role of FSF. Inject responses immediately following the "Enemy Action" described.

- Identify any decision support templates from the perspective of the FSF elements.

- Capture initial elements into WARNO#3.

Operations Order. Prepare to detail and brief for the subordinate Commanders and their staffs.

- Prepare and publish full Appendix (FSF) to Annex C (Operations) to OPORD with appropriate Tabs. For example:

- Tab A (Laydown of Iraqi Security Force in Sector)

- Tab B (Iraqi Army Division Task Organization Chart)

- Tab C (Iraqi Army Operational Readiness Ratings)

- Tab D (S-TT Laydown)

- Tab E (KLE Guidance for 1-3 BCT Leaders Working With ISF)
- Tab F (Iraqi Army Pay Chart)
- Tab G (Iraqi Army Rank Structure)
- Tab H (MoD Org Chart)
- Tab I (MoI Org Chart)
- Tab J (DBE Org Chart)
- Tab K (FP Org Chart)
- Tab A (Laydown of Iraqi Security Force in Sector)
- Tab B (Iraqi Army Division Task Organization Chart)
- Tab C (Iraqi Army Operational Readiness Ratings)
- Tab D (S-TT Laydown)
- Tab E (KLE Guidance for 1-3 BCT Leaders Working With ISF)
- Tab F (Iraqi Army Pay Chart)
- Tab G (Iraqi Army Rank Structure)
- Tab H (MoD Org Chart)
- Tab I (MoI Org Chart)
- Tab J (DBE Org Chart)
- Tab K (FP Org Chart)
- *Brief: FSF Lay down & Advisor coverage up front and follow-up later with "Concept of Support to Advisors" (task, purpose, MoP, MoE per element); Detailed composition and capabilities at each echelon (Division, Brigade, Battalion, etc).*
- Source and follow-up on critical training requirements.
- Answer RFIs from subordinate units.
- Capture initial elements into FRAGO#1 within 2 hours of the OPORD.

During Operations. As part of the battle rhythm, the FSF Planners should:

- Lead SFA Working Group.
- Participate in assigned working groups, offering the FSF perspective (Red Cell, Targeting, Prosecution, Sustainment, etc).

Appendix C

SFA/FID Imperatives

LTC Mark Ulrich from the US Army/Marine Corps Counterinsurgency Center at Fort Leavenworth, Kansas compiled an exceptional list of SFA imperatives based upon the Special Operations Forces imperatives as applied to advisors. Use this table as a baseline for understanding the mindset of a unit assigned to a SFA mission prior to designing the campaign plan. In this table, Host Nation Security Forces (HNSF) is used in lieu of the more widely accepted Foreign Security Forces (FSF) term. The meanings are synonymous.

IMPERATIVES	DESCRIPTION/TENETS	ACTIONS
Understand Operational Environment	<ul><li>Understand US command relationship (both military and interagency)</li><li>Understand the Population (Who, what, when, where, why, and how)</li><li>Understand the Enemy and other Anti-government forces (crime, militias, gangs)</li><li>Understand the higher Commander's Intent</li></ul>	<ul><li>Define relationship as partnership or augmentation</li><li>Conduct analysis using ASCOPE</li><li>Analyze Enemy Order of Battle/Threat Analysis</li><li>Protect the population</li></ul>
Recognize Political Implications	<ul><li>Actions by the U.S and HN forces have legal and political restrictions/implications</li><li>Establish and/or enforce rules of engagement policy</li><li>Understand short and long term political effects</li><li>Human rights are critical for tactical and strategic success.</li><li>Events are reported to US population in real time through mass media. Press are a part of the operational environment</li><li>Events directly impact public opinion locally, in the US, and internationally that can directly affect the mission.</li><li>Insurgents conduct operations for the purpose of political implications among the local populace, external actors, and the US/multinational civilian public support.</li></ul>	<ul><li>Include rules of engagement (ROE in the planning and brief backs of operations</li><li>Include local government leadership in operations</li><li>Reinforce human rights briefings and training to all HNSF Prepare all U.S and HNSF to talk with the press</li><li>Prepare information engagements for all operations</li><li>Anticipate and neutralize the methods enemy forces pass propaganda.</li></ul>

Facilitate Interagency Activities	• Counterinsurgency and Security Forces Assistance (SFA) is both a military and an interagency effort. • Understand the scope and limitations of each agency's influence and programs. • Interagency efforts have a greater impact than any purely military program. • To be successful the active cooperation of the HNSF is normally required. • In irregular warfare unity of effort refers to military and civilians agencies working together.	• Include interagency members in planning and training as appropriate. • Provide assistance to support limited agency resources which can allow them to prioritize their primary roles. • Conduct regular coordination meetings to synchronize military effort to support agencies and agency efforts which support the security situation. • Include HN agencies whenever including US agencies
Engage the Threat Discriminately	• The use of overwhelming firepower though apparently useful in the short term but ultimately plays into the insurgents hands, alienate the population, and turn them away from the HN government • Training and advice to HNSF should be based on the mission and threat. Impact is as much a consideration in selecting training and advice as are the political implications of the type of subject and assistance given. • Targeting insurgents, criminal activities (lawlessness), or subversion, to avoid alienating the populace being defended. • Populace and resources control (PRC) measures, in particular, must be carefully weighed for potential gain versus potential cost. Minimize use of force in important. • Ensure that ROE and escalation of force (EOF are balanced between force protection and safeguarding civilians	• Take civilians into account when considering weapons systems and techniques when planning operations • Include civilians in risk assessment during mission planning • Train and rehearse ROE/ EOF to prepare soldiers to react in accordance to policy. • Publicize reasons for use of PRC (e.g. a curfew is for protection) or enemy propaganda and rumor will dictate the psychological response of the populace. • Update ROE & EOF periodically • ROE/EOF reflects engaging targets that are visually verified and not simply suppressive fire in populated area

Consider Long-term Effects	<ul><li>Counterinsurgencies and Security Force Assistance efforts are inherently long-term. Their goal is to build up the HNSF and assist to alleviate the root causes of the current situation, not just treat the symptoms.</li><li>Understanding the problem in its broader political, military, social and economic context.</li><li>Tactical victories are of little value unless they contribute to the overall operational scheme. The operational scheme to which they relate may be nonmilitary in nature. Military measures are inherently short-term and directed against the symptom (e.g. insurgents) and not the root cause.</li><li>Policies, plans, and operations must be consistent with national and theater priorities and the objectives they support.</li></ul>	<ul><li>Understand local grievances and underlying issues.</li><li>Interact with all aspects of the population and government to identify root causes.</li><li>Ensure commander's intent remains focused on higher goals and policy related to addressing root cause, protecting the local population as well as against insurgents.</li><li>Monitor and update ROE as local government and police gain control of rule of law. Conduct operations that adhere to local laws as possible.</li><li>Understand legal and political constraints (rules of engagement) to avoid strategic failure while achieving tactical success.</li></ul>
Ensure Legitimacy and Credibility of Operations	<ul><li>Reinforce and enhance the legitimacy and credibility of the HNSF and government.</li><li>Trust and credibility gives advisors and US forces legitimacy with the local population which helps divide the threats (e.g. insurgents, criminals, gangs) with the population.</li><li>Legitimacy is the most crucial factor in developing and maintaining support in theater, in the U.S and internationally.</li><li>Without legitimacy and credibility, operations will not receive the support of the local population, the US populace, and the international community.</li></ul>	<ul><li>Conduct joint / multinational patrols and operations.</li><li>Ensure information engagement (IE) is common in all operations and proactive to maintain credibility.</li><li>Engage the media with host nation to inform as well as justify actions.</li><li>Focus on what the population considers the root causes not based on US perspective.</li><li>Develop long-term solutions to restore / improve basic services with HN leaders</li></ul>

Anticipate and Control Psychological Effects	• All operations (i.e. PRC) measures, combat operations, and civic action) have significant psychological effects. • Tactical victory may be negated or overshadowed by negative psychological effects. • Perception of the people may be more important than reality.	• All operations are developed, analyzed and executed with proactive IE. • Continue to gauge the psychological effects with the local population, local government and security forces as well as the enemy (propaganda and interrogation)
Apply Capabilities Indirectly	• Teach planning to the HN instead of giving them tasks. • Successful combat advisors support the US efforts enhancing the legitimacy and credibility of the HN government and security forces. • Balance between controlling the HN unit to ensure tactical operations are successful and not applying enough pressure to HN forces if their efforts are not sufficient to accomplish the mission. • Primary role of combat advisors and partnering units is to advise, train, and help host nation forces take the lead in the fight and to stabilize the HN. • An advisor is not the HN unit commander nor should the advisor accept the HN's lack of effort or high levels of corruption under the excuse that it's their unit.	• Conduct training of host nation forces to teach basics; transition to mentor and advisor during planning and operations to encourage HN to take lead. • Advisors use discretion when advising counterparts as not to embarrass HN leadership. • Advisors should use HN methods whenever possible.

Develop Multiple Options	• The nature of SFA, Counterinsurgency, insurgency, IW, etc is the unexpected. • Plan to use the full range of capabilities. • The operational environment may dictate a change of ROE or type of operations. • Ensure HNSF are capable of shifting from one option to another before and during mission execution (i.e. raid to SSE to follow-on target to talking with the population).	• Continue to refine and train on battle drills and contingencies • Develop an understanding of skills and abilities of the members of the unit and community. • Illicit the input of HN personnel on how to address situations to widen the options beyond conventional techniques. • Include government agencies, special operations, NGOs, local police, HN government to develop additional methods or options of problems.
Ensure Long Term Sustainment	• Avoid advising and training host nation forces in techniques and procedures beyond their capabilities to sustain. • Modify techniques, tactics, and procedures, training, operations, and sustainment to fit the culture, educational level, and technological capability of the host nation forces. • Develop hand-over and sustainment in economic, social, political, and military/ security initiatives and projects. • US funded programs are counterproductive if the populace becomes dependent on them and funding subsequently is lost.	• Understand and utilize the equipment and manpower present in the HN unit's inventory. • Assess capabilities of HN security forces of the military and police for: Leadership, Training, Sustainment and Professionalization • Recognize the programs that are durable, consistent, and sustainable by the host nation. • Avoid programs beyond the HN's economic or technological capacity.

Provide Sufficient Intelligence	• Intelligence forms the basis for all IW activities and programs. Detailed, near-real-time, all-source tactical intelligence products. • Operations also depend on detailed and comprehensive intelligence on all aspects of the operational environment and its internal dynamics. • Human Intelligence, urban recon, and internal security elements which can assess the internal threats, warn the government, take action to penetrate the instability, and assist in neutralizing it. • In assessing the enemy threat consider aspects of the society not directly related to the tactical combat situation. • The information from intelligence assets allows them to advise, train, and help host nation counterparts and ease interagency efforts.	• Combat Advisors and partnering units ensure HN conduct operations using accurate, real-time intelligence. • Combat advisors personnel establish priority of effort when identifying intelligence requirements • Advisors assist HN to prioritize and focus CCIR to receive timely and specific intelligence. • Assess other organizations that impede rule of law and government functions (gangs, criminals, smugglers, militias, mercenaries, organized crime, drug lords and narco-terrorists)
Balance Security and Synchronization	• Partnering units often conduct planning, intelligence, and contingencies unilaterally due to security concerns, but compartmentalizing can exclude key HNs from the planning and learning process (unity of effort) • Insufficient security may compromise a mission, but excessive security will usually cause the mission to fail because of inadequate coordination. (e.g. between the local armed forces and police) • Excluding aspects of the HN due to OPSEC concerns will not lead to sustainment. • The HN may not provide intelligence due to internal security or due to lack of US intelligence support.	• Encourage combined planning, preparation, and operations with HN military, police, and governmental units. • Combat advisors must resolve these conflicting demands on mission planning and execution • Employ measures to mitigate risk of OPSEC instead of dismissing the HN government, police, or military needed for the overall effort. • Advisors must constantly strive to gain the trust of the local HN and population to gain the most HUMINT and support from the HN unit regarding information.

Appendix D

Cliff Notes for Deploying BCT with an Advise and Assist Mission

Colonel (Ret) Rick Everett of the Center for Army Lessons Learned (CALL) compiled a comprehensive list of maxims for Brigade Combat Team (BCT) and Task Force Commanders as a "sanity check" when preparing to conduct a SFA mission.

- Advise and Assist (AA) describes a mission and not a Task Organization.

- Stability Operations are a core competency on the same level of importance with Offense and Defense in Full Spectrum Operations.

- BCT Commanders should select best qualified to serve in Advisory/ Partnership role.

- Mission success is defined as FSF success, no US operational success will compensate for failure of a FSF.

- SFA is now the decisive operation in OIF and OEF.

- Pre-deployment Site Survey (PDSS) should be used to fill Commander's Critical Information Requirements (CCIR) and Friendly Forces Intelligence Requirements (FFIR) gaps with information about the Contemporary Operating Environment (COE), resident population within the Operational Environment (OE) and the FSF.

- BCT Commanders have the flexibility and responsibility to task organize the external

- Augmentation (Use own resources first; then request augmentation)

- Plan for a reserve (QRF).

- The BCT (with augmentation) could be partnered with as many as three FSF Division equivalent units during your rotation.

- Create a perception of success within your OE.

- Host Nation Forces in Lead and US/Coalition Forces in Support.

- Treat the host nation population like you would expect your family to be treated under similar conditions.

- More than likely, you will not own the battle space you occupy.

- Information Operations (IO) must be factored into every operational and second that third level effects considered.

- Non-governmental Organizations (NGOs) and US Government agencies can be enablers to the BCT.

- Leader engagements are the key to success in an AA mission.

- Maintain personal high standards and demand the same from subordinates.

- Be prepared to change your approach with the situation. The enemy has a vote in the outcome.

- Continually assess the situation and the mission both the focus and vision may change.

- Know the difference between leadership and management.

Security Force Assistance (SFA) is the unified action to generate, employ and sustain host nation security forces in support of a legitimate authority (FM 3-07, FM 3-07.1). SFA occurs within the framework of Full Spectrum Operations (FSO). In most situations, involving assistance there is limited offensive and defensive operations involving US forces. SFA describes a mission not a task organization.

SFA may occur as part of multiple operational themes, however, it is more likely to occur during peacetime military engagements, peace operations or irregular warfare.

Successful SFA operations will work seamlessly with the host nation government at levels from the ministerial to the tactical to include entry level training.

The BCT's success or failure may be determined by who is selected to advise and mentor FSF. Those selected should possess the same leadership and staff skills as those selected for command and principle staff positions. They not only represent the BCT the United States Army and the American people as well.

Glossary of Terms

AA – Augmented Advisor (US force)

AAB – Advise and Assist Brigade (US force)

ANA – Afghan National Army (Afghan force)

ANP – Afghan National Police (Afghan force)

ANSF – Afghan National Security Force (Afghan force)

AO – Area of Operations

ASCOPE – Areas, Structures, Capabilities, Organizations, People and Events

AWT – Air Weapons Team (normally US attack helicopters)

BCKS – Battlefield Command Knowledge System (US military website)

BCT – Brigade Combat Team (US force)

BCT-A – Brigade Combat Team – Augmented for Security Force Assistance (US force)

BN – Battalion (military unit)

BTT – Border Transition Team (US force)

CA – Civil Affairs

CALL – Center for Army Lessons Learned (US force)

CMO – Civil-Military Operations

COE – Contemporary Operating Environment

CoIST – Company Intelligence Support Team (US force)

COIN – Counterinsurgency

CONOP – Concept of the Operation; Contingency Operation

DBE – Department of Border Enforcement (Iraq force)

DoD – Department of Defense (US)

DoS – Department of State (US)

EOD – Explosive Ordinance Detachment (US force, normally conducts bomb disposal)

ERU / ERB – Emergency Response Unit / Emergency Response Battalion (Iraq force)

ETT – Embedded Training Team (US force in Afghanistan)

FAS – Functional Area Specialist (US force)

FSF – Foreign Security Forces

GoA – Government of Afghanistan

GoI – Government of Iraq

HNSF – Host Nation Security Forces

HN – Host Nation

HTT – Human Terrain Team (US organization)

IA – Iraqi Army (Iraq force)

IE – Information Engagement

IFP – Iraqi Federal Police (Iraq force)

INP – Iraqi National Police (Iraq force)

IO – Information Operations

IPS – Iraqi Police Service (Iraq force)

IPP – Iraqi Provincial Police (Iraq force)

ISF – Iraqi Security Force

IW – Irregular Warfare

JCISFA – Joint Center for International Security Force Assistance (US organization)

JFCOM – Joint Forces Command (US organization)

JSOC – Joint Special Operations Command (US organization)

JSOU – Joint Special Operations University (US organization)

MEDEVAC – Medical Evacuation (normally conducted by rotary wing assets)

MiTT – Military Transition Team (US force)

MoD – Ministry of Defense (Iraq)

MoI – Ministry of Interior (Iraq)

MWD – Military Working Dog Team (US force)

NPTT – National Police Transition Team (US force)

OE – Operating Environment

PMO – Provost Marshal Office (US force)

S-TT – Stability – Transition Team (US force)

SFA – Security Force Assistance

SOP – Standing Operating Procedure

TACSOP – Tactical Standing Operating Procedure

TCP – Traffic Control Point

TOC – Tactical Operations Center

TTP – Tactics, Techniques and Procedures

UAS – Unmanned Aerial Surveillance (US force)

UAV – Unmanned Aerial Vehicle (US force)

Bibliography

Center for Army Lessons Learned (CALL), *Combat Advisor's Handbook*, Fort Leavenworth, KS. Department of the Army, 2008

Congressional Research Survey (CRS) *Report on Army Specialized Units*, Washington, DC: CRS, January 2008

Joint Center for International Security Force Assistance (JCISFA), *Commander's Handbook for Security Force Assistance*, July 2008

Joint Center for International Security Force Assistance (JCISFA), Security Force Assistance *Planner's Guide for Foreign Security Force Development*, 2009

Osanka, Franklin Mark, ed. *Modern Guerrilla Warfare—Fighting Communist Guerrilla Movements*. New York: The Free Press of Glencoe, a Division of the Macmillan Company, 1962.

Potter, Stubblefield and Monday, *Ambush*! Boulder, CO: Paladin Press, 2010

US Army, Advise Foreign Forces, ARTEP 31-807-33 *Mission Training Plan*, Washington, DC: Department of the Army, 1984

US Army, *Counterinsurgency Operations*, Field Manual 3-24, Washington, DC: Department of the Army, 2006

US Army, *Guerrilla Warfare and Special Forces Operations*, Field Manual 31-21. Washington, DC: Department of the Army, 1961.

US Army, *Military Assistance Training Advisor (MATA) Handbook*. Fort Bragg, NC. The United States Army Special Warfare School, 1964.

US Army, *Security Force Assistance*, Field Manual 3-07.1, Washington, DC: Department of the Army, 2009

US Army, *Advisors Handbook for Stability Operations*, Field Manual 31-73, Washington, DC: Department of the Army, 1967

US Army, *Special Forces Advisors Handbook*, Training Circular 31-73, Washington, DC: Department of the Army, 2008

US Army, *Tactics in Counterinsurgency Operations*, Field Manual 3-24.2, Washington, DC: Department of the Army, 2009

US Army, *Unconventional Warfare Devices and Techniques*, Technical Manual 31-200-1. Washington, DC: Department of the Army, 1966.

About the Author

Lieutenant Colonel Joshua Potter is a US Army Officer who has served in several operational assignments in CONUS, Europe, and South Western Asia. Upon graduating from West Point in 1993, he served in a variety of Air Defense Artillery, Special Forces, and Civil Affairs assignments. He also earned a Master's of Science degree in Health Sciences from Touro University in 2009. Potter co-authored several professional articles, blogs, and sections of military Field Manuals relating to influence techniques, counterinsurgency, and Security Force Assistance. Some of his written sections are included in the Combat Advisor Handbook (2008), FM 3-07.1, SFA (2009), and FM 3-24.2, Tactics in COIN (2009). He also co-authored *Ambush!: A Professionals Guide to Preparing or Preventing Ambushes* (Paladin Press, 2010) with CDR (ret) Gary Stubblefield and Mark Monday.

In accordance with his duties, Potter has advised and partnered with military forces in Saudi Arabia (1994, 1995, and 1997), Republic of Georgia (2000), Russia (2004), Bulgaria (2004), and Iraq (2003-2006, 2009-2010). Specifically, he trained scores of Advisor Teams preparing for Iraq and Afghanistan while stationed in Fort Riley, Kansas from 2007 to 2010. Potter has led teams which trained more than 12,000 deploying military and civilian advisors in the US and 22 supporting countries at the NATO Joint Forces Training Center, Poland as well as 50 Afghan officers and soldiers. He has further developed humanitarian demining operations with Georgian, Armenian, and Azeri military and civilian engineers in 2000.

He earned three Bronze Stars and a Joint Commendation Medal for his multiple tours of service in combat. Among other decorations, Josh earned the Purple Heart when he was wounded by a 60mm mortar attack in Iraq in August 2006. He went on patrol the following day with his 11-man Team and the Iraqi National Police in the streets of Baghdad. During that particular tour of duty (2005-2006), his Team conducted over 300 mounted and dismounted patrols, nabbed over 90 insurgents with his small US Team and 700-man Iraqi National Police Battalion, and personally discovered and secured six IEDs and VBIEDS allowing EOD personnel to destroy them in place. All of his US Team returned home with honor More than 50% of them returned to Iraq and Afghanistan for subsequent tours of service.

In 2009-2010, LTC Potter most recently served as the US Advisor to staff Major General Ali Jassim Muhammed Hassan Al-Firaji, the Commanding General to the 17th Iraqi Army Division, on his fourth combat tour to Iraq (2009-2010). On this tour he was a Stability – Transition Team (S-TT) Chief, assigned to Colonel Roger Cloutier, Commander for 1st Brigade, 3d Infantry Division ("Raiders") and attached to Lieutenant Colonel Greg Sierra, Commander of Task Force 2-7 Infantry, ("Cottonbalers").

He is currently serving as as the Commander of the 81st Civil Affairs Battalion in Fort Hood, Texas.

He is married to Tracey, a woman of singular grace, patience, and charm who raises their blessed three children – Damon, Peyton, and Bradyn while he is away.

www.ingramcontent.com/pod-product-compliance
Lightning Source LLC
LaVergne TN
LVHW061327060426
835511LV00012B/1908